D0746762

MARILYN
Mon Amour

ANDRE DE DIENES

MARILYN
Mon Amour

**The private album of
André de Dienes,
her preferred photographer**

St. Martin's Press • New York

MARILYN MON AMOUR. Copyright © 1985 by André de Dienes.
Copyright © E.P.I. Filipacchi. All rights reserved. Printed in
United States of America. No part of this book may be used
or reproduced in any manner whatsoever without written
permission except in the case of brief quotations embodied
in critical articles or reviews. For information, address
St. Martin's Press, 175 Fifth Avenue, New York, N.Y. 10010

Library of Congress Cataloging in Publication Data
De Dienes, André, 1913—
    Marilyn, mon amour.

    1. Monroe, Marilyn, 1926–1962—Portraits.
2. Moving-picture actors and actresses—United States—
Portraits.   I. Title.
PN2287.M69D4   1985   791.43′028′0924   [B]
85-30745
ISBN 0-312-51504-9
ISBN 0-312-03862-3 (pbk)

First published in France by E.P.I. Filipacchi.
10   9   8   7   6   5   4   3

CONTENTS

André de Dienes
snapped by Marilyn in 1945

THE VERY BEGINNING

So much has been said and written about Marilyn Monroe's death in Hollywood during the night of 4–5 August 1962. All kinds of theories have been put forward: was it too many sleeping pills? Suicide? Murder? Nothing has been proved.

Ever since, some of her closest friends have asked themselves these questions over and over again, no one more despairingly than André de Dienes. He arrived home that night to hear the shrill, insistent ringing of his telephone behind the locked front door. In his haste to answer it, he dropped his keys and once inside, just as he went to grab the receiver, the phone stopped ringing. None of his friends and family or business acquaintances had tried to call him. So the painful, unanswerable question remained: had Marilyn tried to call him for help one last time? He would never know.

André knew Marilyn better than almost anyone. He met her in 1945 and had taken the first photographs of her. She trusted him totally, the man who had loved her so and had been such an unswervingly faithful friend.

André de Dienes is a famous name in the world of photography. His work has appeared in publications all over the world; he will always be considered a master of the artistic nude study. He died on 11 April 1985, aged seventy-one.

On the threshold of old age, he decided to recapture those fleeting moments of his youth which he had once lived with such intensity close to a woman he never stopped loving, to re-live them through the memories and pictures in this album. He was waiting impatiently for the book to be published but that happiness was denied him. He has left this intimate legacy, ensuring that these early moments in Norma Jeane–Marilyn's life are not forgotten.

André de Dienes was born in Transylvania in 1913; but at the end of the First World War that country was handed over to Romania. Like many of their countrymen, his family wanted to remain Hungarian. André was one of eight children in a family ruined by inflation, and some of his earliest memories were of the handfuls of worthless banknotes which he was given to play with.

Faced with this difficult, almost hopeless state of affairs, his mother sought refuge in a village, taking her younger children, including André, with her; the older children went with their father to Budapest where he tried to recover his fortunes. André's mother found the separation and upheaval hard to bear and became ill. During the night of 1 May 1925 she got up to fetch a drink of water, fell into the well and was not found until next morning.

André was only twelve. He was a sensitive, nervous little boy and suffered from nightmares; he felt terribly alone and abandoned in spite of the affection of his indulgent uncle and strict grandmother. He attached himself to the family's young servant girl, Krisztina, a lively, merry creature who thought of him as a mischievous little innocent, as an accomplice for her escapades. Saying they were going to pray at his mother's tomb, she used to take him on long walks through the forest to the village of Turia. Her real purpose was to visit the chapel bellringer, a strange man who lived in the bell tower, surrounded by old books. He would say disturbing things which the little boy did not always understand, predicting that André's fortune awaited him far away, in the land of the setting sun and, pointing to a double 'MM' on a page in a book of illuminations, made him spell out a Latin phrase: *Memento mori* (Remember the dead), and told him that those two Ms would play an important part in his life. Dusk fell; it was time for the angelus. The sound of the bell would awaken the owls, asleep in the thick shadows of the trees. André felt strangely stirred, uneasy. What could Krisztina want with the white-whiskered, long-haired bellringer? In the midst of his confusion he sensed that it had to do with a mystery which the future would reveal to him, sooner or later.

The land of the setting sun . . . that must be America, where the people of dismembered, bankrupt central Europe longed to go. André's uncle had told him tales of brave settlers who had made their fortunes there, the gold rush, the great stretches of land inhabited by Red Indians. The young boy had a feeling that his future lay over there. He said nothing and patiently planned his journey. First, he decided to join his father in Budapest. He was not going to set off on the spur of the moment, as a runaway: it was a considered decision. To be sure of success, he started to go for long hikes and was often away from home; by the time his uncle realized he had gone, André was already well on his way. Gradually he drew nearer to his goal, travelling in a peasant's cart, stealing rides on freight trains, but most of the time on foot. For nourishment he depended on apples stolen from orchards or shared a hobo's scraps of food. Nothing could stop him – not even his increasing exhaustion, thirst and hunger. He believed in his lucky star.

André finally found his father who was still beset by money worries. So André, who was just fifteen, immediately set about earning his living. Starting as an errand boy, he soon became a clerk in a silk shop. This modest job did at least enable him to discover a world of beauty, luxury and women of which he was never to tire. An elegant Parisienne taught him the rules of French grammar and gave him a very thorough grounding in the rules of love; he was fascinated by the female body and tried his hand at painting, only to be discouraged by his lack of talent.

It was at this point that he discovered photography: at last he knew what he wanted to do. Without any help, he developed his own technique, experimenting with unusual lighting and angles, enthusiastically inventing new variations on an ever-recurring theme: the female body. When there was no live model available, he photographed statues.

At the age of nineteen he left Hungary. The first stop on his westward journey was Paris. Here he associated with journalists and Bohemians like himself and earned his living by selling photographs to magazines. These photographs, taken here and there, of news stories or on his wanderings, were notable for the fresh eye they cast on ordinary, everyday things.

hese were the interwar years; full of surprises, miracles. One afternoon when he was idly taking pictures of a winged horse in the Place de la Concorde, an elegant woman approached him: would he agree to photograph, there at the foot of the statue, the slim young girl who was with her? She was a mannequin from the salon of the highly fashionable Parisian couturier Molyneux.

This photograph was enough to launch him as a fashion photographer. He was inventive and daring; everyone wanted him. He revelled in the money, the gorgeous girls, the sophisticated society ladies. He had a talent for happiness, endless energy, and an insatiable appetite for life. After Paris came other capital cities: Rome, London . . .

But somehow this was not enough. *Vogue* offered him a Hollywood contract. He accepted, but made his way there slowly. He wanted to see the Indians, the ones he had seen in the picture books his uncle had given him so long ago in Transylvania. He visited the pueblos of New Mexico, toting a backpack, his cameras slung round him, carefree. At the end of his journey Hollywood welcomed him with open arms.

The coming of war meant even more opportunities for him. By this time he was a naturalized American, but was exempt from military service because of an inflammation of the inner ear – which was never to give him any trouble. He earned his bread and butter by taking photographs for enormous illustrated mail-order catalogues, working freelance and treating himself to long trips all over America between assignments.

Everything interested, attracted and delighted him. He built up a collection of photos taken for his own pleasure and approached his nude studies like a painter or sculptor, making a ray of light caress a curve here, throwing another into relief with a touch of shadow. His dream was to see the nude make the transition into high-class, glossy publications.

Then Hollywood would summon him once more and each time he returned. The girls were so beautiful! He knew how to talk to them, understand them and make them even more beautiful. Each photo session was an adventure: they would go off to the beach, the cliffs or a ranch. By now André had enough self-confidence to turn down any contracts he found too onerous. He could suit himself. He was expensive: three hundred dollars a day, but the girls who posed for him were almost certain to appear on the cover of *Gala* or *Look* during the months which followed; girls like Linda Christian, Ruth Roman, Yvette Mimieux, Jane Russell. The years slipped by unnoticed.

Some things, however, did not work out: a failed marriage was followed by an expensive divorce. He had to move to New York. He discovered a double studio in an old apartment building, just off Broadway, installed a dark room and office and furnished it throughout with things he had brought back from his travels.

He took on fashion work and advertising assignments, and improved his technique in nude photography. Sometimes his search for models had unexpected results: on one occasion a half-starved girl he had picked up in a square robbed him; another had a miscarriage in his apartment. His independence cost him dearly: he had to say goodbye to some of his treasures; a sculpture; a carpet. But he did not lose heart; he still had faith in himself.

However, André had had enough of taking bathing beauty shots under his shower and having his neighbours below complain about the damage done to their ceiling by these sessions. He longed for the great outdoors, wide open spaces, walks along the sands, waves. One day he decided to take his model to Long Island where the beach was bound to be deserted in the middle of the week. His model agreed and thoroughly enjoyed herself, playing a guitar, her hair blowing in the wind. After a while a very distinguished-looking middle-aged man came up to them. He had binoculars round his neck: a voyeur? He hoped they did not mind, he had been watching the young lady taking up her poses from his window in Montank Manor which overlooks the beach. The wind was getting chilly and he thought he would come to say hello and bring along a bottle of whisky and some glasses.

They chatted. Their charming host eventually invited both photographer and model to join him for dinner 'in that great barrack of a place' where he was bored to death. A friendship sprang up which had some surprises in store.

For some time André saw a good deal of his new friend, going places with him, inviting him back to the studio; he admired him for being cultivated, for his taste and discernment; his well-cut suits, silk shirts and shoes from the best shops. One day, however, this agreeable companion revealed that he lived in a small studio. He had only been a guest at the magnificent mansion of Montank Manor, having stayed on after the weekend!

André was tactful enough not to ask questions and instead confided that his own career was at a standstill.

'Well, of course, California is where your future lies.'

This was said so unequivocally that André was taken aback.

'Take it from someone who really knows, that is where you will find what you've always been looking for. Not just success but the most important thing in your life.'

Did he have second sight? They consulted the tarot cards and these confirmed what he had said. The double 'MM' ran like a golden thread through the fabric of André's destiny.

So he went back to California. His friend rented his apartment from him for four months, paying in advance. André loaded his cameras and equipment into his Buick and set off, not knowing that ahead lay a fateful meeting which would seal his destiny.

I said to Norma Jean : " Sit on the highway, it represents Life!
                                              You have a long way to go!!"

It all started here,
in 1945. Norma Jean
was 19; just started
modelling. This was
her first professional
assignment. I was mad-
ly in love with her, and
wanted to take many,many
pictures of her.
Why I wanted that, it's
a long story,yet to tell.

While photographing this,
looking at the tiny little
white stars on her red
skirt, unconsciously, I
began prognosticating
to her,that she
will become very
famous ! That those
littel stars meant
great fame ! Yet,

I had no idea
why I said that!
It just happened !

ANDRE DE DIENES

purpose was to visit the chapel bellringer, a strange man who lived in the bell tower, surrounded by old books. He would say disturbing things which the little boy did not always understand, predicting that André's fortune awaited him far away, in the land of the setting sun and, pointing to a double 'MM' on a page in a book of illuminations, made him spell out a Latin phrase: *Memento mori* (Remember the dead), and told him that those two Ms would play an important part in his life. Dusk fell; it was time for the angelus. The sound of the bell would awaken the owls, asleep in the thick shadows of the trees. André felt strangely stirred, uneasy. What could Krisztina want with the white-whiskered, long-haired bellringer? In the midst of his confusion he sensed that it had to do with a mystery which the future would reveal to him, sooner or later.

The land of the setting sun . . . that must be America, where the people of dismembered, bankrupt central Europe longed to go. André's uncle had told him tales of brave settlers who had made their fortunes there, the gold rush, the great stretches of land inhabited by Red Indians. The young boy had a feeling that his future lay over there. He said nothing and patiently planned his journey. First, he decided to join his father in Budapest. He was not going to set off on the spur of the moment, as a runaway: it was a considered decision. To be sure of success, he started to go for long hikes and was often away from home; by the time his uncle realized he had gone, André was already well on his way. Gradually he drew nearer to his goal, travelling in a peasant's cart, stealing rides on freight trains,

but most of the time on foot. For nourishment he depended on apples stolen from orchards or shared a hobo's scraps of food. Nothing could stop him – not even his increasing exhaustion, thirst and hunger. He believed in his lucky star.

André finally found his father who was still beset by money worries. So André, who was just fifteen, immediately set about earning his living. Starting as an errand boy, he soon became a clerk in a silk shop. This modest job did at least enable him to discover a world of beauty, luxury and women of which he was never to tire. An elegant Parisienne taught him the rules of French grammar and gave him a very thorough grounding in the rules of love; he was fascinated by the female body and tried his hand at painting, only to be discouraged by his lack of talent.

It was at this point that he discovered photography: at last he knew what he wanted to do. Without any help, he developed his own technique, experimenting with unusual lighting and angles, enthusiastically inventing new variations on an ever-recurring theme: the female body. When there was no live model available, he photographed statues.

At the age of nineteen he left Hungary. The first stop on his westward journey was Paris. Here he associated with journalists and Bohemians like himself and earned his living by selling photographs to magazines. These photographs, taken here and there, of news stories or on his wanderings, were notable for the fresh eye they cast on ordinary, everyday things.

these were the interwar years; full of surprises, miracles. One afternoon when he was idly taking pictures of a winged horse in the Place de la Concorde, an elegant woman approached him: would he agree to photograph, there at the foot of the statue, the slim young girl who was with her? She was a mannequin from the salon of the highly fashionable Parisian couturier Molyneux.

This photograph was enough to launch him as a fashion photographer. He was inventive and daring; everyone wanted him. He revelled in the money, the gorgeous girls, the sophisticated society ladies. He had a talent for happiness, endless energy, and an insatiable appetite for life. After Paris came other capital cities: Rome, London . . .

But somehow this was not enough. *Vogue* offered him a Hollywood contract. He accepted, but made his way there slowly. He wanted to see the Indians, the ones he had seen in the picture books his uncle had given him so long ago in Transylvania. He visited the pueblos of New Mexico, toting a backpack, his cameras slung round him, carefree. At the end of his journey Hollywood welcomed him with open arms.

The coming of war meant even more opportunities for him. By this time he was a naturalized American, but was exempt from military service because of an inflammation of the inner ear – which was never to give him any trouble. He earned his bread and butter by taking photographs for enormous illustrated mail-order catalogues, working freelance and treating himself to long trips all over America between assignments.

Everything interested, attracted and delighted him. He built up a collection of photos taken for his own pleasure and approached his nude studies like a painter or sculptor, making a ray of light caress a curve here, throwing another into relief with a touch of shadow. His dream was to see the nude make the transition into high-class, glossy publications.

Then Hollywood would summon him once more and each time he returned. The girls were so beautiful! He knew how to talk to them, understand them and make them even more beautiful. Each photo session was an adventure: they would go off to the beach, the cliffs or a ranch. By now André had enough self-confidence to turn down any contracts he found too onerous. He could suit himself. He was expensive: three hundred dollars a day, but the girls who posed for him were almost certain to appear on the cover of *Gala* or *Look* during the months which followed; girls like Linda Christian, Ruth Roman, Yvette Mimieux, Jane Russell. The years slipped by unnoticed.

Some things, however, did not work out: a failed marriage was followed by an expensive divorce. He had to move to New York. He discovered a double studio in an old apartment building, just off Broadway, installed a dark room and office and furnished it throughout with things he had brought back from his travels.

He took on fashion work and advertising assignments, and improved his technique in nude photography. Sometimes his search for models had unexpected results: on one occasion a half-starved girl he had picked up in a square robbed him; another had a miscarriage in his apartment. His independence cost him dearly: he had to say goodbye to some of his treasures; a sculpture; a carpet. But he did not lose heart; he still had faith in himself.

However, André had had enough of taking bathing beauty shots under his shower and having his neighbours below complain about the damage done to their ceiling by these sessions. He longed for the great outdoors, wide open spaces, walks along the sands, waves. One day he decided to take his model to Long Island where the beach was bound to be deserted in the middle of the week. His model agreed and thoroughly enjoyed herself, playing a guitar, her hair blowing in the wind. After a while a very distinguished-looking middle-aged man came up to them. He had binoculars round his neck: a voyeur? He hoped they did not mind, he had been watching the young lady taking up her poses from his window in Montank Manor which overlooks the beach. The wind was getting chilly and he thought he would come to say hello and bring along a bottle of whisky and some glasses.

They chatted. Their charming host eventually invited both photographer and model to join him for dinner 'in that great barrack of a place' where he was bored to death. A friendship sprang up which had some surprises in store.

For some time André saw a good deal of his new friend, going places with him, inviting him back to the studio; he admired him for being cultivated, for his taste and discernment; his well-cut suits, silk shirts and shoes from the best shops. One day, however, this agreeable companion revealed that he lived in a small studio. He had only been a guest at the magnificent mansion of Montank Manor, having stayed on after the weekend!

André was tactful enough not to ask questions and instead confided that his own career was at a standstill.

'Well, of course, California is where your future lies.'

This was said so unequivocally that André was taken aback.

'Take it from someone who really knows, that is where you will find what you've always been looking for. Not just success but the most important thing in your life.'

Did he have second sight? They consulted the tarot cards and these confirmed what he had said. The double 'MM' ran like a golden thread through the fabric of André's destiny.

So he went back to California. His friend rented his apartment from him for four months, paying in advance. André loaded his cameras and equipment into his Buick and set off, not knowing that ahead lay a fateful meeting which would seal his destiny.

I said to Norma Jean : " Sit on the highway, it represents Life!
You have a long way to go!"

It all started here,
in 1945. Norma Jean
was 19; just started
modelling. This was
her first professional
assignment. I was mad-
ly in love with her, and
wanted to take many,many
pictures of her.
Why I wanted that, it's
a long story,yet to tell.

While photographing this,
looking at the tiny little
white stars on her red
skirt, unconsciously, I
began prognosticating
to her, that she
will become very
famous ! That those
littel stars meant
great fame !   Yet,

I had no idea
why I said that!
It just happened !

ANDRE DE DIENES

1

PRELUDE

When I arrived in Hollywood I called a special agency. I wanted a model who would be prepared to pose in the nude if necessary. I felt slightly irresolute, almost hesitant. Yes, they did have a young girl on their books who had no experience but was eager to start. She might accept my conditions. They would send her along. An hour later she was at my door: she was wearing a skimpy pink sweater, her curly hair tied with a ribbon to match, and carried a hat box. She seemed unsure of herself. With her childlike smile and clear gaze, she was absolutely enchanting.

I had years of experience behind me. I could weigh up a woman's beauty at a glance, her presence and style, and whether she was photogenic. There was no need to take her clothes off to know what she was like underneath. At first sight she did not look anything like what I was after: much too naive, too awkward. Perfect no doubt for those silly, sentimental postcards, posing with a bunch of flowers or a kitten. But I immediately felt how much I could draw out of her still childlike face, from her well-rounded yet coltish body, from this unpolished beauty.

'My name is Norma Jeane Baker,' she said.

She wore a wedding ring which seemed absurd: she was nineteen but looked much younger. She had, however, already been married for three years to a man named Dougherty who sailed the high seas. They were in the process of getting divorced. She accepted my rate

The first page in André's album. He knew at once that this enchanting nineteen-year-old would go far

of pay without arguing, the usual price: a hundred dollars a week, but I was to pay for any props or accessories, extras, transport and food if we did any location photography. She was free at the moment so we could start the next day.

I was impatient to train the camera on her, to choose the right light to set off her skin and her hair, to capture her expression, to make her move, run, stand still, arch her back, stretch. I wanted to catch hold of whatever it was I sensed lay behind that candid smile, those blonde curls and the pink sweater. In one fell swoop I was intrigued, moved and attracted by her.

Seeing her, I recalled a childhood memory which had signalled the approach of a world of enchantment, then still unknown to me: the realm of femininity with all the joys it lavishes upon those who understand it. Krisztina, with her plaits and white apron, was a young servant girl whom my grandmother ruled with a rod of iron. One summer's day, when I was about twelve, I came upon her bathing naked in a big wooden tub by a barn. She smiled at me without the slightest embarrassment. After all, I was just a young child to her; or was she in fact aware of her fascination for me and amused by it? I felt the same allure when confronted by Norma Jeane. She could not have guessed it: I was just friendly, detached, a real pro. I could tell that she felt reassured, happy to have found a job, her first ever. From now on she would at least have a reference, since my signature was a recommendation in itself. Better still, her photos would be published in the best American and foreign magazines.

Love,
Norma Jeane

She listened to me like a little girl being told the story of Cinderella. Everything about me surprised her. The room I had showed her into was nothing like an ordinary hotel room: I never travel without taking a few of my pictures, books and odds and ends with me. She was disconcerted to see that instead of having photos of fashion models or film stars on my walls, they were of a peculiar tribe of Indians, the Seminoles, who live in the mangrove swamps of Florida. I had spent some time among them and brought back a fascinating record of my stay.

She listened to me attentively. Suddenly she came down to earth: 'Excuse me, do you want to see me in my swimsuit?'

The two-piece she took out of her hat box did not do her justice. It did not matter, it revealed what I had already surmised: firm, well-rounded breasts, a trim waist set off by the perfect curve of her hips; long, lithe legs. And now I could see the quality of her skin: smooth, polished, the type which reflects light instead of absorbing it. I could not help stroking it very lightly. I wished I had a powerful projector to flood it with light. But I had not bothered to book a studio at the Garden of Allah, the movie people's favourite hotel. I had come to California to work out in the open, going against the prevailing fashion which had produced an endless supply of over touched-up studio portraits devoid of any personality.

Was he trying to recapture his first childhood love for Krisztina by dressing Norma Jeane as a little Hungarian peasant girl?

NORMA JEAN DID NOT WEAR JEANS I BOUGHT IT FOR HER,

PUBL. IN "MARILYN" 1973

Norma Jeane was the ideal model for what I wanted to do, and she agreed without demur to my request for an early morning start. I wanted to make the most of the clear morning light which gently strokes the curve of a shoulder, tinges blonde hair with silver and makes the eyes sparkle without dazzling them.

i had picked a beach which I knew would be deserted at that time of year. But I could not wait. I wanted Norma Jeane there and then, in the freshness of the early morning. I wanted her barefoot, natural, without make-up. She danced in the sunshine, laughing, whirling round, prancing, sinking to the ground, getting to her feet again, supple as a cat, brimming over with the joy of living. I took shot after

She was a sweater and skirt girl; her first pair of jeans were a present from André – and she wore them with style

shot of her, happy to feel her blossoming with each succeeding photograph. All at once, I felt quite certain that this little ragamuffin in her schoolgirl skirt would go far.

That evening, as I watched the prints appear in the developing bath in the lab, the predictions of my friend and of the bellringer of Turia crossed my mind; I shut them out, happy to be alone with her, far from Hollywood with all its razzmatazz, intent upon capturing a woman's beauty against a superb natural backdrop. I felt Norma Jeane trusted me. On the beach, between poses, she had drawn a heart in the wet sand. It was her way of thanking me for the opportunity and freedom I had given her. She had most probably been dreading the thought of the demands and pressures of a fashionable photographer. With every picture I became more convinced of her great future – and more determined to do some extended location work with her.

But first we had to seek permission from an aunt with whom she was living in a Hollywood suburb. She was a reserved, timid woman, knowing nothing of the frenetic world into which her niece was about to tiptoe on her pretty feet. Aunt Anna asked us to lunch. I won her over very quickly, telling her how I had photographed Dorothy McGuire on a cliff top and Ingrid Bergman in a field of ripe wheat. I also told her about Shirley Temple, half-woman, half-child, whom Norma Jeane resembled, with her mass of curls, peach complexion and uncontrollable fits of giggling. So enchanted had I been by Shirley that I had briefly entertained thoughts of marrying her, only to be promptly discouraged by a

Diones

huge Great Dane chained to the railings of her garden barking at me!

Aunt Anna readily gave us her blessing once she knew I would see that there was everything in the Buick to make her niece as comfortable as possible; that I would take care of providing her wardrobe, both for the journey and when posing for me. According to each model's type of beauty, I liked to vary my props. I had stupidly left two beautiful big soft toy rabbits behind in New York which would have come in useful to underline the ambiguity of Norma Jeane's naive but disturbing charm. I went from shop to shop with her, spending my money recklessly.

One morning we were ready at last. Norma Jeane had not even bothered to find out where we were going. Since I hate being tied down, I was delighted. On the outskirts of Hollywood I was flagged down by the police. I had, according to them, repeatedly veered over the centre line, probably because I was intoxicated. Norma Jeane was boiling with indignation: not only was I stone cold sober, I had not even committed any offence. It would be a real crime to fine me.

The traffic cops listened to her with a twinkle in their eyes; she had obviously won them over. They let us off for twenty dollars. Firemen, politicians, millionaires . . . Marilyn's charm never failed.

As we covered the first lap of our journey she slept, curled up in her seat like a kitten; I thought that it would not take long for me to uncover the secret of her charm: after all, a camera is like a third, all-seeing eye. But I had forgotten that love is blind!

She was a completely
unknown girl in 1945,
but while I took this
picture below, I said to
Norma Jean:"You will become
the world's most photographed
beauty; and when I will be old,
I shall write stories about
women, and you.... "
I did not know why I spoke
like that; but strangely --
it all came through, just as
I told that to her.(in Dec.1945).

(THIS BAFFLED ME EVER SINCE!)

TWO FOR THE ROAD

We drove through a desolate landscape, the sky lowering and stormy at times, although it was December. I had decided to make straight for the Mojave Desert, crossing Death Valley. I had a full tank of gas, the trunk was packed with provisions and the back of the car had been turned into a sleeping compartment with mattress, blankets and pillows. There were plates, cutlery and vacuum flasks in the picnic hamper. Gradually the gas stations grew more infrequent. Not a single roadside café for a sandwich or a cool drink. Norma Jeane took it all in her stride. Every so often she would sink her teeth into an apple, consume a jar of cottage cheese and, when she was tired, fall asleep like a baby in the middle of my stories about her brilliant career and the fame which lay in store for her. Did she believe me?

I felt almost as if I had kidnapped her. Which I suppose I had. I wanted her all to myself because I longed to make her my mistress. Hardly surprising. An intimacy develops between a photographer and his model which often means that a long photo session ends in bed or, failing that, on the grass or on a sandy beach. Norma Jeane still had something of the schoolgirl about her and had dutifully joined in saying grace at her aunt's. On the other hand she had been married, and was no prude, laughing heartily when I told some rather dirty stories. So why not?

What with our picnics and chats, interspersed with

Late in 1945 André and Norma Jeane took to the road for over a month, travelling thousands of miles through California, Arizona, Nevada and Oregon

my daydreams at the wheel and her restorative catnaps, we had soon reached the middle of the desert. I had spotted a place called Darwin Falls on the map, which I thought would be perfect for my planned re-creation of Ingres' famous painting, 'La Source'. The light was good. A suitable pretext for asking my passenger to undress and pose in the nude. I was a little anxious as there was no time to lose: after the burning heat of the day, the desert would soon turn icy cold. I was impatient to get there, not least because I wanted to take this opportunity to do an 'Eve before the Fall' as well.

Among my assorted props I had a long rubber snake which I planned to curl round a branch. I did not quite know how I was going to ask Norma Jeane to pose naked. I felt both impatient and diffident, equally afraid she would agree too readily or refuse. After driving round in circles, we finally reached the famous falls on foot . . . to find it had dwindled to a trickle of water. The earthly paradise of my imagination was no more! No forbidden fruit for us to share, only a faded sign: 'Beware of snakes!' And there in the sand one could indeed make out some disquieting tracks. I coolly assured Norma Jeane that snakes hibernate and never come out in winter. She pretended to believe me. Furious and disappointed, I slung my make-believe snake over a bush with its head resting on the sign. And photographed my Eve fully clothed. Alas, this negative, together with many others, was lost later on during the journey.

That evening I decided we would spend the night at

Furnace Creek, a tourist village in the very heart of Death Valley. Hypocritically, I asked my companion in a studiedly natural tone whether I was to book one or two hotel rooms, waiting for her reply with hope and apprehension. She answered with not the slightest embarrassment: it had been a long day and she needed a really good night's sleep to look her best the next day. Just my luck. She was right, of course.

Later, however, sleeplessly turning from side to side in my narrow bed, I told myself I was a fool to be so hesitant, like a lovesick college boy. When I could bear it no longer, I decided to knock on her door. Her face was puffy with sleep but she smiled and calmly asked me to be good and go back to bed, which I did. To my great surprise, I fell asleep at once.

W hen I awoke it was already broad daylight. One of those wonderful desert mornings of transparent light, the outline of the rocks sharply defined against the deep blue sky. My favourite

Sunrise in the heart of Death Valley. Norma Jeane keeps smiling happily as she poses in the bitter cold of a desert dawn

time of day was slipping through my fingers. I threw on my clothes and dashed out, bumping into Norma Jeane who was already dressed and lightly made up. She was in high spirits, laughingly calling me a 'lazy-bones'. This model was certainly not true to type. They usually have to be dragged out of bed after night-clubbing till the early hours. But there she was, fresh as a daisy, wearing a polo neck sweater, slacks and a smile. I just had to photograph her like that, with her tousled hair, surrounded by the rocks and barren landscape. I wanted to encapsulate the contrasting images of youth and life and this desert of death.

I felt I could not photograph her too often that day. We were alone, in a precious solitude, barely disturbed now and then by the silent presence of an eagle hovering high above us. She stretched out on the sand, resting her head in my lap and I stroked her hair. It felt good to be alive. Suddenly the memory of the old bellringer's two Latin words came back to me: *Memento mori*, and my heart misgave me. We were so young, so full of life . . .

My uncle's old stories of gold prospectors kept running through my head. Both for my own pleasure and to entertain Norma Jeane on the long drive, I told her the one about 'Old Dutch', a lone prospector who discovered an inexhaustible seam and managed to take the secret to his deathbed. Many people searched desperately for this miraculous seam, and many of them lost their lives in the process, on what came to be known as 'Superstition Mountain'. Why should I not try my luck? I had a pickaxe and a mattock in the car.

Norma Jeane listened to me while savouring a slice of canned pineapple; licking the syrup greedily off her fingers, she replied: 'Why not?'

Another of my dreams made her laugh when I shared it with her: I wanted to create a blissful oasis in this hostile desert for just the two of us and for the children we would have. We would grow palms, orange trees and pepper plants. She would tame some of the wild donkeys, foxes and skunks and learn how to make real Hungarian goulash. I would trap buzzards and eagles. And take millions of photographs. More laughter. How could she take a man seriously when he assured her she would be a star, talked about finding a lost seam and covering her with gold, then suggested giving her a pack of kids and starting a zoo in the middle of the desert?

By the time we reached Las Vegas night had fallen and it was bitterly cold. We stopped to fill up with gas. All around us the fever of gambling joints, the clatter of one-armed bandits. I suggested to Norma Jeane that she should put a coin in one and hold out her wind-breaker. A stream of coins poured into it. Over ten dollars! She was thrilled, all set to repeat the experiment. I told her very solemnly that one has to be careful with magic; she must wait for another auspicious moment. She bought herself some chewing gum and a few magazines and stoically got back into the car while all around us dozens of hotels offered a good night's rest. As I drove along, I kept reproaching myself. Did I have the right to subject her to such a gruelling and lonely journey? Worn out, I stopped the car and waited for dawn.

We had reached a fantastic location, Cathedral Gorge, a labyrinth of narrow passes hemmed in between high rock faces, eroded by wind and rain; all about us was the sound of rushing waterfalls. The rocks had been worn away and some had come to resemble strange sculptures, leering gargoyles, motionless draperies. Only a photograph could portray the profusion of these seething rocks. And only a nude could provide a fitting contrast for such apocalyptic scenery.

I started to set up my camera, choosing the best frame line. I did not want Norma Jeane to have to take up her pose until the last minute, to spare her the embarrassment of waiting around naked. Just then two rough types suddenly appeared from behind a rock. They suggested they should show us round the gorge. According to them, there might be some nasty surprises in store for us without a guide to show us the way; we had to watch out for the crevasses hidden by the brushwood and beware of dangerous animals. They were the dangerous animals. I sensed it at once. The way they looked Norma Jeane over confirmed my fears. I managed to thank them politely, assuring them that we had not counted on spending any time there, I just wanted to take a few snaps. They moved off with bad grace, taking their time about it. I quickly gathered up my equipment and hurried Norma Jeane towards the car which, fortunately, started up at once.

Neither of us said a word until the Buick reached the highway. It had been a near thing. We might have ended up for good at the bottom of a ravine on a bed of stones. And perhaps one day our bones would have been found and taken for those of a couple of nomadic Indians, dead of thirst or killed by some wild animal. Once more, I felt guilty. Just because I wanted her all to myself, I had exposed her to the risk of being raped by those sinister prowlers, of getting lost among the sand dunes of the desert, of the car breaking down, far from any hope of rescue. Suddenly, one of our tyres burst, making us swerve violently on to the soft shoulder. Norma Jeane offered to help me change the wheel. I would not hear of it. She had to stay immaculate, with no trace of perspiration or grease, ready to be photographed at any time. She sat on a large stone and settled down to wait patiently. All at once I was beside her, thanking her for being there, for trusting me; I wanted to take her in my arms, say I was sorry. I begged her to marry me. I was ready to do anything for her, I loved her. She looked away and said nothing. Was she trying to keep me at a distance without hurting me?

Just then I caught sight of an enormous spider close to one of her feet. The bite of this particular spider can be fatal; at the very least it causes a very high temperature, swelling and burning pains. I know from first-hand experience. But Norma Jeane seemed more intrigued than frightened. She even stretched out her hand. My instinctive reflex was to press the shutter release, to have my camera capture her gesture. This photo was lost as well.

We had a second flat tyre two hours later, near a gas station kept by a woman whose skin was as weather-

193

194

MT. HOOD,
OREGON.
(AFTER A
BLIZZARD
WHAT GOT
US STRANDE
AT "GOVERN-
MENT LODGE

195

196

199

198

197

J

31

ANDRE DE DIENES

beaten as old leather. With a small cigar dangling from her lips, she asked me what on earth we were doing in this god-forsaken spot. I told her that I was making for the Picacho camp near Yuma. She stated calmly that I was mad and asked Norma Jeane in for a cup of tea. Fixing my car took me some considerable time. The two women had a chance to have a long chat. I was then told by the old woman that the spider was a bad omen, that it was getting late and we would not be able to drive on through the dunes. People even got lost in them in broad daylight and a sandstorm was brewing. Besides, she had found out that Norma Jeane's mother lived in Portland and was all on her own after a spell in a psychiatric hospital. Instead of wandering around in the middle of nowhere, it was my duty to drive little Norma Jeane to see her sick mother. I had a good mind to tell this old witch to go to hell and take her sermons with her. Her piercing gaze made me feel uncomfortable. I paid her what I owed her and we got back on the road to Yuma which grew narrower and more winding the further we went, often vanishing under drifts of sand which the wind had blown off the dunes. Suddenly, without Norma Jeane having said anything, I turned the car round. That was it. We were going to Portland.

I was thirty. I was no saint. Norma Jeane and I were living at close quarters, twenty-four hours a day, surrounded by all the paraphernalia of sleeping, eating and dressing in a car. She adjusted easily to all this muddle while it tended to get on my nerves. I had to put up with orange peel on the rear window shelf, Coca-Cola splashes on the windscreen, hair curlers caught between the seats. And in contrast to all this jumble of clothes, magazines and cans of food, there was Norma Jeane, still smiling, relaxed, fresh and glowing, whether just surfacing from sleep or dropping with fatigue. She slept a great deal.

So confident had I been at the outset that this was going to be a dual adventure, both a professional and sentimental journey, that I wanted to give of my best in both senses. I wanted to take my greatest pictures ever while creating some perfect memories for the two of us. Although I wanted her so badly the last thing I wanted was to hustle her into going to bed with me, even though she would acquiesce. I wanted her to be willing.

Portland was well over a thousand miles to the north. I started by driving day and night, more to stay in control of myself than to save time. But I had to allow for a halt before venturing into the Yosemite National Park which I really wanted to see. Merced, the last settlement before the road zigzags up into the mountains, has nothing much to recommend it, particularly if you arrive there in the middle of the night, in icy rain! Among the few hotels, there was only one room free, shabby and seedy. Norma Jeane was exhausted. Even I was suffering from stiff and aching legs, but I did not want to risk soiling my first night of love with her by such squalid surroundings. Without a word, I took her by the hand and led her back to the car. There I settled my passenger as snugly as possible, tucking the blankets and pillows round her. Dawn came at last. It was snowing. Everything was so beautiful that I woke Norma Jeane. The road we were on skirted the edge of a cliff, beside enormous rocks balanced on the edge of the drop, and then cut through silent pine forests. Everything was white as far as the eye could see. We had forgotten how tired we were. Suddenly Norma Jeane stifled a shout: a brown bear was crossing the road. There are lots of bears in the Yosemite forests. They are usually harmless and only attack people if they feel threatened. My companion was only partially reassured. I must admit that I felt relieved when I parked the car outside the best hotel in the valley.

The holiday-makers had arrived for the winter sports, the hotel was fully booked. All they could offer us was a couple of log cabins in the middle of the woods. Their roofs sagged beneath the weight of snow; the air was so cold it seemed to have congealed. There was no heating. A notice informed us that there was a w.c. some way away, behind the cabins. All we could do was to go our separate ways to bed, fully clothed, and tuck ourselves in. In the middle of the night I awoke to a knocking on my door. It was Norma Jeane, wrapped in a blanket and stammering that she wanted to go to the toilet but she was scared.

back home in my village when I was a child I had been told that wild animals can be driven away by noise. I emptied out a large can of tomato juice and escorted poor Norma Jeane, banging a spoon on my tin drum and making a fearful din. It was best to treat it as a joke. The next morning, however, she was still overcome with embarrassment at having disturbed me for such a reason. I knew that a hearty breakfast and a nice hot shower would make her forget the whole affair. So I took her back to the hotel and while she fixed herself up I had a complete winter sports outfit sent up to the room with the finishing touch of a superb Indian belt encrusted with turquoise and silver. When she came out of the shower and saw all these beautiful things, she flushed and her eyes filled with tears. Events had followed hard on each other's heels, so that one minute she was subjected to a gruelling endurance test, the next overwhelmed with joy. But I was impatient to see how her new wardrobe transformed her. We dashed out into the snow, the first she had ever seen. Norma Jeane was thrilled, dazzled by all this beauty and purity. They were unforgettable hours, so intense, so short . . .

That evening, at a run-of-the-mill motel, I asked for two communicating bedrooms. I had decided to try my luck, even though the surroundings left something to be desired. The manageress was suspicious and wanted to know whether we were married. It was no use lying to her, she would only have asked for proof. She demanded ten dollars and held out two keys . . . to separate bedrooms! Incensed, I saw Norma Jeane to her bedroom, shut myself in my own and tried to sleep. Norma Jeane now became the object of my suppressed rage. She let me spoil her, protect her and drive her halfway across the United States, taking it all for granted, 'paying' me with a smile here, a thank-you there and the occasional dewy-eyed look to express how moved or pleased she was. I was an idiot not to try anything!

I wrote her a letter saying how intolerable I found living with a woman I desired without being able to take her in my arms; it was both stupid and cruel because 'only one thing counts in life, Norma Jeane, and that's love. Do you realize that? I'll show you it's true. Come to me. I'm waiting for you. We'll make love. You won't be disappointed. I love you. I'll always love you.' I signed it 'That crazy Hungarian, André.'

then I settled down to wait. It was past midnight before my fit of excitement gave way to anger once more. I cannot bear feeling unhappy. From the nearby bar I could hear a rowdy group of high-spirited night-owls and I decided to join them. I would order a bottle of good wine to share with these strangers and drown my sorrows. Or rather my disappointment. I carry my liquor well but that does not stop me being careful. There was no sense in running the risk of having my pocket book stolen. I hid it under the mattress and left my bedroom.

The next morning, after rather a lively night, I was fast asleep when Norma Jeane came – at long last – and knocked on my door. I packed up my things, not daring to look her in the face. Had she read my letter? Had she actually received it? I might have pushed it under the wrong door in the dark. Best say nothing. My head felt muzzy and the weather was awful: thick fog, a dank-ness which penetrated one's bones. As we reached the outskirts of a small town, I stopped the car outside a cafeteria and ordered a sumptuous breakfast: waffles, maple syrup, cereals, jams, everything on the menu. I enjoyed watching Norma Jeane revelling in the feast, syrup round the edge of her lips. When the time came to pay the check, no billfold! Forgotten under the mattress a good twenty miles away in my motel room and I had left the door open! I always carry a reserve of a hundred dollars in a pocket belt. I pressed these into Norma Jeane's hand and rushed off without stopping to explain. The room had not yet been cleaned and the pocket book was where I had left it. What luck!

The return journey seemed endless, with good reason: the fog had thickened and I took the wrong turning at a crossroads. I drove around in circles, time was passing and I was in danger of running out of gas. What would become of Norma Jeane, abandoned without any explanation and just the hundred dollars? It was past noon when I finally came within sight of the cafeteria. They told me that the young lady had left soon after asking where the bus station was. I tore off. She was telephoning her Aunt Anna to say she was on her way home. The bus was leaving in ten minutes. She fell into my arms, in tears. I hugged her close, kissing her hair, her wet cheeks, trembling, overcome. I had almost lost her.

We covered mile after mile until we came to the edge of a forest of giant sequoias. After the burning, arid desert and the snow-covered mountains we were now surrounded by the enchantment of the tall timberland. The sun was shining once more, filtering through the foliage in long, slanting rays, glancing between tree trunks over three hundred feet tall. The air was full of a strong smell of resin. We got out of the car and felt slightly breathless, a little dizzy with gazing upwards trying to make out the top of the trees, row upon row of them as far as the eye could see.

Norma Jeane had walked a little way away from me and was bending over with the sun behind her to look at a decaying, fungi-covered tree stump, fascinated by an insect crawling along a piece of bark. The backlighting effect turned her hair into a halo and I imagined her naked in this Eden. At that moment she stood up,

holding herself very erect, lost in her own thoughts, her face uplifted towards the patches of sky. All at once I no longer saw the forest as a Paradise but as a vast cathedral. Asking her to pose naked would have been sacrilegious.

That evening both the Buick and I were feeling the strain. I left Norma Jeane at a motel and went to find a garage to have the engine and tyres checked. Portland was not far away now. When I got back to the motel after quite a while, there was no sign of Norma Jeane, in my room or hers. And I soon realized that someone had made the most of our absence: some of my equipment and a valise had been stolen. The loss was grievous. Losing bedlinen and clothes was bad enough but what I really minded was being robbed of a camera and, even worse, an attaché case in which I kept my supply of spare films and several exposed spools. Two emotions warred in me: anger and dismay. Then I heard Norma Jeane's laugh. A car stopped outside the door. She climbed out, weighed down by a bag which the young man at the wheel had handed her. I must have looked pretty unfriendly, since he took his leave at once and drove off.

Norma Jeane seemed utterly nonplussed by my attitude. She had only gone downtown to an Italian grocery store to buy a few things for an Italian dinner: salami, Bel Paese, Chianti. The shop assistant had driven her back, that was all. Her high spirits had evaporated and she listened, crestfallen and on the verge of tears, while I enumerated all the things we had lost because she was such a scatterbrain. Suddenly she flashed back: 'For heaven's sake, André, it's not the end of the world! Most of our things were in the back of the car. It could have been much worse, couldn't it?'

She was right. It was only much later, too late, that I realized that the little impromptu feast was probably the answer to my letter. The true prelude to our night of love.

Norma Jeane's mother lived in an old hotel in the centre of Portland, in a depressing bedroom on the top floor. The reunion between mother and daughter lacked warmth. They had nothing to say to each other. Mrs Baker was a woman of uncertain age, emaciated and apathetic, making no effort to put us at our ease. She did not even seem interested in knowing what exactly my relationship with her daughter was. I stayed in the background, pretending to leaf through an old magazine. Norma Jeane put on a cheerful front. She had unpacked the presents we had bought: a scarf, scent, chocolates. They stayed where they were on the table. A silence ensued. Then Mrs Baker buried her face in her hands and seemed to forget all about us. It was distressing. She had obviously been released from hospital too soon. There was no point in hanging around. I mentioned an urgent appointment and had no difficulty in taking my leave and Norma Jeane with me.

i had to make up for having squandered so much time and money. I had decided to drive out to Timberline Lodge, a very good hotel at the foot of Mount Hood about eighty miles from Portland. I needed gaiety, noise, movement. I wanted to go skiing, eat well, make love. It was raining. I could see that Norma Jeane was depressed. The evening was growing colder, the rain had turned to snow. I extolled the pleasures of a good, well-heated hotel, a soft bed, the joys of skiing. She did not know how to ski. Never mind, I would soon teach her.

I was unable to cheer her up. When we arrived at Timberline Lodge she begged me to drive on, to find a less luxurious hotel. She could not face a lot of people. I hesitated, disappointed. This was the first time she had upset my itinerary. But it was not just a whim. I let her have her way. The snow was falling thick and fast, the road was becoming impassable. I made out some lights shining from an old brick building which rejoiced in the grand name of Government Lodge. We were in luck, there was one room free. Only one. With a double bed. Norma Jeane did not demur. There was nowhere else to go at that time of night and in such weather. To cheer her up, I pointed out the rows of one-armed bandits in the hotel lobby. She pushed her coin into the slot when I gave the word, just like that first time in Las Vegas and again, a deluge of coins poured from the machine. No sooner had I whispered in her ear 'Am I entitled to a small commission?' than she ran over to the bar, calling out to the bartender: 'Give him a drink, it's my round.'

The hotel was old-fashioned but charming; dinner was excellent, the bedroom unremarkable and there was just the one shower in the bathroom. Heads or tails who goes first. She won. As she showered she hummed to herself. She slipped quickly into the big bed, where I joined her. It seemed the most natural thing in the world. The night was ours.

During the journey a familiarity had grown up between us, leaving no room for shyness. In my dreams I had explored her body; reality far surpassed my imagination. Everything she felt for me, trust, gratitude, even admiration, was fused in her surrender. Everything was so simple, so wonderful. Why had we waited, hesitated, denied ourselves so long? Our bodies were so well matched, made for each other. I could not get enough of that silky skin, of her supple body both docile and demanding, of our shared, repeated pleasure and, suddenly, as my cheek brushed hers, I realized she was crying. I was filled with a strange emotion, I felt I was a child again. I was twelve years old once more and it was Krisztina crying silently as she held me in her arms. I had not forgotten that night so long ago when, sensing her heartache over some great misfortune, I sought her out in her garret. She was sobbing into her pillow. I think she must have been pregnant. Not long after, she left the village and I never learned what became of her. With Norma Jeane I discovered the fulfilment and tenderness which two beings can feel, and which no words can express, as they mingle their tears, warmth and sighs.

Heaven was on our side: as we surfaced from the deep slumber that follows love-making, I saw that thick snowflakes were falling fast. The roads would be impassable without special snow tyres. We were prisoners. We spent the whole day in our room, only emerging during a bright spell to take some photos. The light was not very good, or at least that was our excuse to go back to bed. Norma Jeane was playful and provocative, snuggling down among the crumpled sheets, then holding them up as a screen for her naked body, only to throw them back, laughing; she smoothed them meticulously, like a tablecloth, before eating a piece of toast. I could not take my eyes off her. I made a mental note of all the poses I would ask her to repeat when it came to photographing her. The room was not well lit. To have used the flash would have destroyed our intimacy. For that one day, the lover took precedence over the professional photographer. Those blissful moments were mine alone. To let others share them would be a desecration.

She had lacquered her nails and while they were drying she held out her hands to me, palms uppermost. I was surprised and rather disturbed when I made out two capital letters, two Ms, the first letters of those words in the old bellringer's book: *Memento mori*. I brushed the memory away. I stated that 'MM' stood for 'Marry Me'. It was pre-ordained. We had to get married as soon as possible, as soon as she had obtained a quickie divorce in Las Vegas. It all seemed so obvious, inevitable, imperative to us at the time. The wedding night had simply anticipated the engagement. I promised Norma Jeane one of those heavy gold rings worn by married women in my native land.

A wedding calls for a celebration; I ordered up a bottle of champagne. There must be an announcement as well. I asked the operator to put me through to New York. I wanted to thank my friend for pushing me into setting off. There was no reply from my number. I found out from the janitor that he had met a violent death the day before, in a road accident.

A few laconic words from a thousand miles away and my world rocked. Just as I had glimpsed happiness, I had to give it up – at least for the time being. I had to head home as quickly as possible, not least for my cat, shut up on his own in my apartment without food or water. Norma Jeane took my decision very well. I was to take her back to her aunt's home in Los Angeles where she would await my return.

The journey seemed endless. I pondered my black thoughts in silence. Norma Jeane slept. Sleep was always her refuge. When we arrived in Hollywood, it occurred to me that I could lessen the sadness of our parting a little by taking her for a coffee to a famous place she had never been to: Schwab's, the drugstore and daily meeting place for directors, stars, starlettes, reporters and photographers. A lively, entertaining place, just right for making contact with the world again. But why had I waited till the last minute to write the cheque I owed Norma Jeane for her modelling services? She had earned every cent and would need it to live on while waiting for me to get back. I left her in front of the magazine stand and went to find a corner of the counter where I could make out my cheque and sign it. When I came back, she was chatting to a stranger. A stranger to her, but not to me. He was a fellow photographer who had the entrée into all the big studios. He was asking her to pose for him. I was stunned to hear Norma Jeane accept, giving him her address and telephone number.

I had to stop myself making a scene. It would have been ludicrous and unfair. I was going away, unable to say when I would be back. I had spent hours explaining to Norma Jeane that she had everything it takes to become a star; nothing gave me the right to insist that she should go into purdah while waiting for me. But I was tortured by jealousy. Someone else was going to photograph her, tell her how to pose, when to smile. I had enough self-control to say nothing, to hide my feelings, and took Norma Jeane back to her aunt. As soon as I returned we were going to push her divorce through as quickly as possible. By the summer of 1946 we would be married; both of us were going to have meteoric careers. She could be sure of that. Anyway, I was sure.

y return journey to New York was catastrophic. My car gave out before the outskirts of Los Angeles. I got rid of it for eighty dollars, the scrap price, and caught the first train, only to realize, too late, that I had forgotten about my emergency fund of two hundred dollars which I had taken the precaution of hiding inside the hand-grip of the brake. As we sped across the dreary flatlands of the Middle West I added up the total balance of the month's wanderings, crammed with incident and so rich in discoveries. The cost had been high. I had spent over seven thousand dollars on my car, gas, films, clothes and general expenses, not counting the stuff which had been stolen and the dollars I had stupidly left in their hiding place. The photos I had brought back from this zigzag expedition had been taken more for pleasure than with an eye to my job. There was no guarantee that my shots of Norma Jeane had not been damaged during our long tour in extremes of heat and cold, nor that this complete unknown's sex appeal would be apparent to the artistic directors of the top magazines.

I did at least have the joy of finding my cat peacefully asleep on the divan. His litter tray stank but there was still a little food and water left in his bowls. My friend had obviously left him well provided for when he left town, presumably for some days. Everything was tidy. The blankets folded, the dishes stacked, clothes put away in the closets and, in a drawer, the emerald tie pin he often wore, his ruby-studded cufflinks, a gold cigarette case and an old fob watch on a heavy, worked chain. A treasure store. It was as if my friend had wanted to make restitution for the heavy expenses of an adventure undertaken at his behest. Also, under the divan, I discovered a suitcase which contained packs of playing cards and tarot cards and a stack of French banknotes. In a letter addressed to me which I found in the inner pocket of one of his jackets, he wrote that our friendship had been of great comfort to him. He had a premonition of impending death. Sudden, violent. And he bequeathed me everything he possessed, together with some advice: not to live for the pursuit of success, money and fame, but for the only possession which really counts for a man: the love of a woman. He had searched in vain for the right one, who could bring him happiness. He hoped that I would be luckier.

If I were to meet the expenses of Norma Jeane's divorce and start a new life, I would need money. I could certainly earn it fast, but to do so, it was advisable to stay in New York where I had lots of contacts, my work was well known and I would be allowed more freedom than in Hollywood where the studios imposed their methods and taste on everyone. The sale of my unexpected inheritance fetched the seven thousand dollars spent on the trip. I paid six thousand dollars cash for a Cadillac and hired a model whom I photographed nude in the grounds of a friend's house in Connecticut.

I wrote frequently to Norma Jeane, telling her about my activities. Letters from her were few and far between. After a long gap, I would telephone. She almost always said it was difficult to make ends meet. I reassured her, promising to send a money order to see her through . . . till the next call.

The weeks passed. I urged Norma Jeane to go to Las Vegas and speed up her divorce which had been delayed because her husband was still on the other side of the world. Summer had come: sultry, humid and stormy. I had accepted a job which was a routine one for me: the winter catalogue of a large mail order clothing company, Montgomery Ward. I duly set off with ten ravishingly beautiful fashion models. I posed them on the terraces of the best hotels, in sumptuous seaside mansions lent by obliging businessmen. Museums also put their rooms at our disposal. How pleasant, one would think. In fact it was an ordeal for everyone. For the models, sweltering in their mink coats, for the dressers knee deep in suitcases and for me, stumping around, eyeing the light which was too harsh or too overcast, swearing and sweating like a pig under my dark cloth.

Norma Jeane had no way of knowing where to reach me in the evenings when, worn out, I could not face waiting hours for the connection to Hollywood. One day I could stand it no longer and quit without notice. I had reached the end of my tether. I wanted to go to Las Vegas with Norma Jeane, sit tight until she was free and marry her five minutes later. I was risking my professional reputation; I could not have cared less. It was generally thought I was having a nervous breakdown due to overwork. I came out of it well; they even paid me for what I had done so far, including expenses.

I congratulated myself for having had the courage to make *the* decision of my life: to go back to Norma Jeane and devote myself exclusively to taking photos which would reveal the potential I sensed in her, even if it meant starting over, with all the sacrifices my new artistic vocation would entail. I was beside myself with impatience as I waited for my call to Norma Jeane to come through. She must set off immediately for Las Vegas. I would follow the next day. We would meet at such and such a time, place and . . . Only then did she manage to interrupt me for long enough to say softly, no doubt smiling her childlike smile: 'But André, I don't want to get married . . . I want to get into movies.'

A long distance telephone call is no way to have an argument. The most unexpected and cruel blows leave me outwardly surprisingly calm. Wasting no more words, I asked Norma Jeane to meet me six days later at one o'clock in the afternoon, on the corner of Sunset and Vine. I was there. I waited over two hours for her. She did not show up. I should have expected it.

Nevertheless I was worried. Had she misunderstood? Was she sick? An accident? I had encouraged her to rent a little one-roomed apartment at Santa Monica. I was in two minds whether to go there or not. We might miss each other. Finally I decided to take the risk.

As I was parking, I saw a man coming out of the apartment building and immediately I was convinced he had been to see Norma Jeane. I waited until he had got into his car and driven off. Then I went and knocked on her door. She opened it unsuspectingly and grew pale. She had obviously not taken my arrival seriously, nor our meeting. Or she had got the wrong day. She clutched a black lace negligée more tightly round her; underneath she was naked. I made my way into a cluttered room, very untidy; records, photos and stockings lay on the floor, a crumpled dress on a chair. There were dirty glasses and an empty bottle on the table. And a bed, rumpled.

Norma Jeane seemed stunned. She hovered behind me while I looked for somewhere to sit. I even managed a wry smile. I had lived in Paris, Berlin, Rome. And had my share of adventures. I had no intention of telling her off, nor of making myself look ridiculous by showing how jealous I was. She eyed me, sniffling. Was she afraid or ashamed? I managed to make light of it. She was quite right not to want to marry someone like me, a wandering gypsy, tyrannical, moody and a sex maniac to boot. You have to steer clear of these central Europeans. I laughed, and by now she was laughing with me, almost reassured. She did not love me any more? She was free, I had no hold over her. I knew only too well the role played by the casting couch in her chosen career.

I left her with a friendly, conspiratorial kiss. She could always count on me. Deep down, I was in a state of shock. I bought two bottles of whisky and took the road to the cliffs. I knew where to go, where they dropped sheer into the sea from a dizzy height. The alcohol would soon take effect. A touch of accelerator and the Cadillac would take a deep dive . . . and me with it.

evening came, one of those ineffably beautiful sunsets with scudding purple, slate and blue-grey clouds, under-lit by the last rays of the sun as it sank into the sea. Picture postcard stuff, perhaps, but exquisite. Instinctively I reached for my camera, got out of the car and focused. Suddenly, all that mattered was that I should capture this fleeting moment of beauty. I had not touched the whisky, but I had sobered up after being drunk with despair.

I turned the car round and headed back to Los Angeles.

FIRST PHOTOS
OF
MARILYN
MONROE.

THE LEGEND
HAS STARTED....

AT SAN JUAN CAPISTRANO MISSIO
1946
(SHE IS WEARING MY GOLD
WRIST WATCH.)

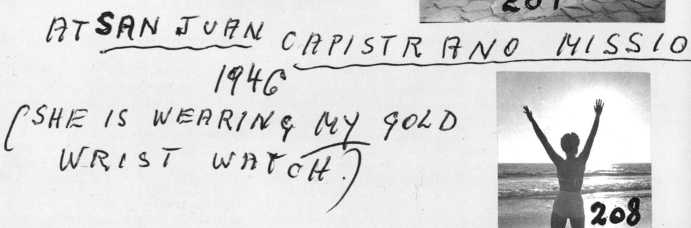

1946

J 33

ANDRE DE DIENES

METAMORPHOSIS

I was scrupulous in keeping my promises to Norma Jeane. From then onwards I was just a good friend to her. A brother? Deep down, perhaps. A broken love affair can sometimes bind two people more closely than ties of blood. We would never be strangers.

After that moment of madness which nearly had me jumping off the clifftop, I was in control of myself again. How could I ever have dreamed of keeping her jealously to myself, after my original, immediate conviction that a glittering future awaited her in a world so alien to the kind of love I had dreamed of?

I never called on her again without being asked. But I was always ready to listen when she wanted to confide in me: her hopes, her strivings, her disappointments. Sometimes we did not see each other for months. Then one fine day she would call me up, often because she wanted me to take some more photos of her. Anyone starting out in that type of career needs a plentiful supply of extremely varied poses for selections to leave with the agencies, studios and magazines. I refused to think of the succession of men who might be part of my pretty friend's life. I threw myself into my work – building up my collection of nudes – and into casual affairs.

I wanted to retain my status as Norma Jeane's favourite photographer. In that area I considered I had no serious competitors. Whenever we met for a session I continued to mould my model. Her hair was a paler blonde than before and she now knew how to make-up. More important, I taught her how to make the most of herself, how to project herself, to put herself across in public. Never to set foot outside her door unless she seemed on top form, head held high, a smile on her lips, however tired or discouraged she really felt. Thanks to me, she discovered her best profile, toned down her laugh and learned how to stand up, sit down and hold out her hand, all done with the utmost propriety and provocativeness.

I persuaded her to be seen everywhere, never to say no to photographers. Not like those stuck-up little madams who dodge the camera or insist on first knowing where the photo will appear. All that mattered was that people should see as much of her as possible. Rita Hayworth and Betty Grable had been pinned up in soldiers' barracks, sailors' quarters and night-clubs. Their pictures had circled the globe. Hers were becoming well known. It was time to find her a name.

Her divorce had finally come through but her maiden name, Baker, was very unexciting. Also, her christian names, Norma Jeane, were hardly star material. It was high time she acquired a new identity. Several of my photos taken during our trip had appeared in the top magazines; people were starting to recognize her but she was still anonymous.

In late summer 1946 the name was chosen. She telephoned to ask me to come to see her at once. What did I think of this name: Marilyn Monroe?

'Well, don't you like it?'

'It isn't that.'

The name sounded great. It was easy to imagine the letters in blazing lights on the front of a cinema. The studio people who had thought it up were experts and it was best to trust their judgment. But both names began with an M . . .

'You really think the two Ms will bring me luck?'

She had picked up a pencil and was trying out her signature with two large, curly, romantic Ms on a notepad. She was getting acquainted with her new identity, saying 'Marilyn Monroe' as if tasting a piece of candy.

From then onwards no one was allowed to call her by any other name. Not even me. I shut the two of us away in the past, turned the lock and threw away the key. Marilyn did the same. During the years which followed, while her brand-new name grew larger on the billboards and became imprinted on the public's consciousness, she was to answer hundreds of questions about her childhood, her likes and dislikes, her love affairs and her heartaches without false modesty; never did she so much as mention our madcap escapade.

She was still having an uphill struggle, with the occasional walk-on part, a burlesque song in the chorus, but she was still one of a crowd; options were not renewed, what mediocre contracts she did land led nowhere. But she kept trying. One of her films had a premonitory title *Dangerous Years* – for Marilyn was to live through a period that was both dangerous and difficult. Only much later was it known how desperate she had been. People were shocked that she had posed nude for a calendar but she simply had not known where her next meal was coming from. I never guessed all this. She had her pride.

She went to drama school where they discovered she had a thin little singing voice. One or two suggestive ditties which she sang in *Ladies of the Chorus* in 1948 brought her to the notice of a few critics, but neither Fox nor Columbia thought it worth their while to sign her up.

In spite of everything she did not forget our lessons and put a good face on things. She automatically took up the right stance for the photographers, pushing out her breasts, giving a slight sideways slant to her hips, an inviting smile and sparkling eyes. With a few twinges of jealousy I accepted that I would have to share her with my fellow photographers. But I was the only one to spot the infinitesimal changes which were gradually transforming Norma Jeane into Marilyn underneath her carefree manner.

From time to time I would persuade her to escape from the confined world of Hollywood; during these carefully planned getaways I took her to visit the old Spanish missions dating from the arrival of Christianity in California. Their white walls, silent chapels and paved cloisters echoing to our footsteps, the gardens

"PEACE OF MIND"

"A HYMN TO THE SUN"

"SELF-TORMENT"

"THE END OF EVERYTHING"

(WITH THIS SAD, SORDID EXPRESSION 39
NORMA JEAN PROPHESIZED HER DESTINY.)
(16 years before her
death
1962

ANDRE DE DIENES
1401 SUNSET PLAZA DRIVE
HOLLYWOOD, CALIF. 90069

with box hedges and crosses standing out against the blue sky, evoked a response in her.

I took her to Valentino's monument where she picked one of the roses blooming there and noticed that he had died in 1926, the year she was born. She protested when I told her that those 'whom the Gods love die young' and declared that she wanted a long life even if she never became famous, but she had a feeling that hers would be short.

As I broadened her horizons I brought up more serious subjects, introducing her to poetry through selected quotations. A line would often strike a chord within her, she would repeat it, and I knew she was committing it to memory; I noticed she remembered the saddest ones: 'Life is a fragile shell' or 'Fame is the bright mourning of happiness'.

She was twenty and had never experienced the intoxication of success, yet already there was a shadow over her radiance, in her laughter.

One day when we were relaxing on the beach between photo sessions, I decided to capture some new expressions I had glimpsed on Marilyn's face. Getting her in close-up, I asked her to react instinctively, without giving herself time to think, to the words happiness, surprise, reflection, doubt, peace of mind, sadness, self-torment . . . and death.

When I said 'death' she took hold of the folded dark-cloth and covered her head with it. Death to her was blackness, nothingness. I tried to coax another reaction from her. Death might be a beginning, the hope of an everlasting light. She shook her head: 'That's what death is for me.'

She turned towards me, her face set and despairing, eyes dulled, her mouth suddenly bereft of colour. To her, death was 'the end of everything'.

I filed these poignant photos away under that year: 1946. For a long time I forgot all about them. Perhaps this strange interlude of introspection upset Marilyn; she asked me to take her back to Hollywood as quickly as possible, she had an important dinner date. Did she want to blot it all out?

It was not all sweetness and light between us. Sometimes I would get angry with her for thinking I should come running when she needed me, only to be forgotten for weeks on end when she was otherwise engaged. She often resented unsolicited advice. One day I went so far as to complain that she had thrown my life into chaos with her whims. She retorted crisply that she had never asked me for anything, quite the reverse, she had always been too submissive. The last sparks from a love affair, brief and violent as a thunderstorm, which was to leave its mark on me for ever.

Enthralled by the new expressions glimpsed on her face, André asked Marilyn to interpret a succession of emotions, ranging from ecstasy to despair

Here — she is
No more
"Norma Jean"
This is the
young,
happy —
Marilyn Monroe, just at the brink of fame !

SUMMER — 1949

257
258
259
260
261
262
260/A
W
263
264
265
266
267
268
269

SAME PHOTO !

ANDRE DE DIENES
1401 SUNSET PLAZA DRIVE
HOLLYWOOD, CALIF. 90069

FASCINATION

t was Groucho Marx who, in 1949, gave Marilyn her first real break. This moustachioed faun had only to look at a pretty woman through those big glasses and it was as if they revealed and magnified whatever sex appeal she possessed. *Love Happy* is far from being the four brothers' best film but the figure which Marilyn cut in it tickled the public's fancy nearly as much as Groucho made them laugh.

That summer I had gone back to New York to carry out some urgent assignments. I had made my mark in illustrated magazines with my nudes whose beauty alone had won them recognition. They were a far cry from the scenes showing varying stages of undress and indecency in certain underground publications. My reputation was growing. My photos often made the covers of the best magazines – on 16 February 1947 a photo of Norma Jeane–Marilyn, taken on our trip in 1945, was on the front of *Parade*.

I had agreed to go to Pennsylvania, at the invitation of the president of Ansco, a big roll film manufacturer. The New York summer was at its height with the usual stifling, unhealthy humidity. Sleep was impossible. I might as well set off and drive through the night to Binghamton where Ansco had its headquarters. Once on the road I was gradually overcome by a sort of torpor, only to realize that I had taken the wrong feeder road and was now calmly heading towards New York! I might as well postpone my interview with my impor-

On the threshold of fame: the Marx brothers' Love Happy *has brought Marilyn her big chance. Here she is, excited and happy, on Tobey beach not far from New York*

tant customer until a later date. All I had to do was telephone. And it was the telephone which roused me from the deep sleep I had sunk into on getting home. A clear, joyous, insistent voice, close at hand: Marilyn! She was at the Pierre, one of New York's most luxurious hotels.

'André, isn't it great, I always told you my day would come! This is it. I'm on my way!'

Mary Pickford, who had produced Associated Artists' *Love Happy* had decided to launch the film with a promotional tour. So, for the first time in her life, Marilyn found herself in New York where the film was being premièred the next day.

'I've got the whole day off tomorrow. We could take lots of photos, I'm really going to need them, the studio ones are so . . . so conventional.'

Once more I had been requisitioned and, as usual, it did not even occur to me to refuse. What about all my work? It would just have to wait.

I rushed out to a department store and bought two swimsuits, one pink, one white; two parasols, one plain, one spotted, and several large coloured scarves. Knowing my favourite model's appetite, I also prepared a lavish picnic. We had arranged to set off early, before the heat haze blanketed the city. At seven o'clock the telephone rang: she was ready and waiting. I shall never forget my surprise when I saw her step out of the hotel elevator: she had the presence and ease of an established star, accentuated by her innate grace. She was radiant, exhilarated by Groucho Marx's encouragement, the prospect of a long tour all over the

United States and with renewed confidence in her future. And, who knows, perhaps she was also looking forward to spending the day with me?

I took her to a beach about eighty miles from New York which was, unfortunately, already crowded with bathers. The sky was clouding over. What with all those people and the ominously dark sky, it looked as if my day was going to be ruined. As we arrived at Tobey beach the storm broke, violent, blinding. Everyone fled to take shelter in their cars. Half an hour later the beach had been left just to the two of us, alone on the shore beneath a clear sky.

Marilyn seemed to have boundless energy, going in and out of the water, playing with the few props I had brought along, inventing all sorts of effective poses with them. Her bosom had filled out since our last expedition and the swimsuits were a little tight. They pinched the upper curve of her breasts but she did not complain; she changed out of the wet swimsuit and pulled on the dry one, screened by one of the large scarves. I hoped for a gust of wind, to blow the thin material aside so that I could capture a picture of her naked body, but no friendly breeze came to my assistance. What happened that day was more unexpected . . . more wonderful.

I used to have a little Persian cat who went everywhere with me and at the last minute I had slipped him into his travelling basket. He was a sort of talisman. I adore cats and this one got as bored without me as I did without him. He had slept until then but eventually ventured out onto the beach, intrigued by the cool sand, the waves advancing and retreating. He amused Marilyn and she started to imitate his sinuous movements. The game had something of a dance about it.

'Go on, dance for the cat. As if you wanted to seduce him.'

She swayed, feline, provocative. The contrast of her mischievous and childlike laugh, her hair blowing in the wind with the lascivious way she moved, accentuating every curve of her body, was unbelievably exciting.

throughout that long day we were happy just being together in the dazzling summer sun. And we had not wasted our time. Thanks to the cat, Marilyn had discovered her irresistible walk. Ansco bought the entire set of photos I had taken of her without quibbling over the price. The next day her film was premièred. New York fell in love with Marilyn, and after New York, America and the whole world followed. Perhaps fate had willed that I should take the wrong turning on the way to Binghamton so that I could spend a day in Paradise, when the new Eve was born.

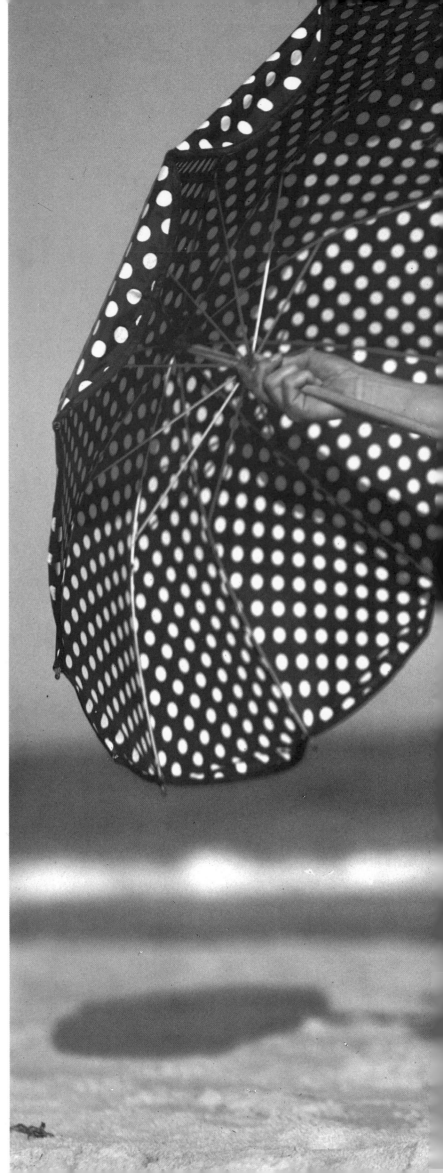

1952

WITH
NATASHA
LYTESS,
HER
ACTING
COACH.

1953

IN THE
BUNGALOW;
"HOTEL
BEL AIR",
WEST
LOS ANGELES.

MARILYN
WAS THE
HAPPIEST
WOMAN IN
THE WORLD..
SUCCESS,
FAME, WAS
COMING
TO HER...

STARDOM

Marilyn was now filming non-stop, playing adorable idiots in *The Asphalt Jungle*, *Love Nest* and *Clash by Night*.

She co-starred with some of the great actresses of contemporary cinema: Bette Davis, Barbara Stanwyck. All the studios were chasing her. She was on the threshold of stardom.

I had decided to make my permanent home in California where the climate and the constant, stimulating sense of something always going on suited me. I had bought a secluded house on a hillside swarming with lizards, where one had to be careful not to tread on a scorpion and sometimes the coyotes could be heard howling at night. This was at the very beginning of the 1950s. Today it has vanished beneath serried rows of apartment buildings.

I found the atmosphere of the house conducive to work. I had set up my own photographic laboratory there, together with all my archives. In January 1952 everything, or nearly everything, was swept away by a landslip in the wake of a tornado. Any sensible person, I suppose, would have abandoned the flooded house with its cracked walls and mudpatch of a yard. Sick at heart I threw whole boxes of sodden negatives into a pit I had dug in the yard. Nevertheless, I refused to admit defeat and gradually built up my precious collections again.

Despite the hectic pace of her meteoric career,

Gentlemen prefer blondes ... Marilyn gradually became more and more of a blonde, while André remained as captivated as ever by her effervescence and sparkle

Marilyn often came to see me. She enjoyed meeting such vintage stars as Harold Lloyd who was very keen on photography and also a good friend of mine, helping me to shovel the rubble from my ruined house, or Mario Lanza, then at the height of his fame. My home was also a haven of peace for her. She could relax there, feel free to collapse into helpless giggles with me once more and forget her everyday worries. She used to do the cooking and we would listen to operas. A little drunk on music and Beaujolais, I would pour the last few drops of the wine over her feet, pretending it was the perfumed oil with which the ancients anointed the feet of their guests.

One day we had worked non-stop from morning onwards. I had even decided not to answer the telephone although it kept on ringing. I had taken some photos of Marilyn in a foam bath. She was warming herself by the fire, wrapped in a large bath towel. She would provocatively draw it aside only to cover herself again while peeping up at me through her eyelashes. I pretended not to notice. It was a game. In the end it was she who grew tired of the sound of the telephone and lifted the receiver. She was being sent for. I saw her grow pale.

'I must go,' she said in a toneless voice.

She dressed quickly, in silence. I could not get a word out of her. Only the next day did I learn, together with the rest of Hollywood, that three years earlier – before the Marx brothers' film had brought her the first worthwhile role of her career – Marilyn had been paid fifty dollars to pose nude for a photographer called

674

675

673

676

D

678

680

O

677

681

682

682

687

688

687

683

679

J

686

645

685

684

85

ANDRE de DIENES
1401 SUNSET PLAZA DRIVE
HOLLYWOOD, CALIF. 90069

Tom Kelley. This controversial photo had appeared in a calendar. It caused a furore. Most Hollywood scandals are damaging. Marilyn's career was still at a delicate stage and for a little while it looked as if it had been blighted. But, strangely enough, far from ruining Marilyn, the 'calendar affair' made her – 1953 was her big year.

She thought she had found happiness when she married Joe DiMaggio. He was charming, famous and very rich; for a few months I hardly saw anything of her. But she was not entirely lost to me. For there she was on the cinema screen. In *Niagara*, wearing a slinky red dress, she reverted to the voluptuous rhythm of the cat walking on Tobey beach. A year later, in *River of No Return*, her first western, she was back in the sun-baked desert of our wanderings in Death Valley (could it really be ten years ago?). In *The Seven Year Itch* I rediscovered her legs, revealed by the draught from the ventilator grille. And *Bus Stop*? A filmed repeat performance of the scene at the cafeteria when she thought she had been abandoned on the road to Portland.

By 1956 she had divorced DiMaggio and, to everyone's surprise, married Arthur Miller. The millions of people who had become her fans, who admired and loved her – for she inspired as much tenderness as desire – saw only her breasts, her hips, her legs and her innocent, still childlike face. How could they ever comprehend this young woman's thirst for knowledge, or picture her as a conscientious, enquiring and humble student, who had so often been my attentive listener, as deeply moved by the lines of Omar Khayyam as by Violetta's death in *La Traviata*? To them she was the wife of a famous writer, welcomed and made much of everywhere; her every film was a success. How then could they guess that she also knew the bitterness of personal failure? Failure in *The Prince and the Showgirl*, when Laurence Olivier's harsh verdict condemned her for not acting like Vivien Leigh. A more profound failure when the baby she had longed for and was carrying so happily never came into the world. Her tears. Her lassitude.

She came to see me one evening, muffled up in a coat and scarf. She looked unwell and admitted she could no longer sleep. I could see her in my mind's eye, cradled by the pillows while the Buick jolted along the bumpy roads, sleeping like a baby. I wanted to ask her what was really the matter? What sorrow, what trouble tormented her? How long was it since she had made love spontaneously, light-heartedly?

She was huddled in an armchair, bewilderment in her eyes, when a model I was expecting rang the doorbell. Marilyn looked panic-stricken. Darkness was falling. I did not turn on the lights. The girl came in; she looked sensational, her hair and make-up beautifully done, a pencil-skirted close-fitting dress clinging to the outline of her breasts, waist and legs, so tight that she had to take small steps, while swaying her firm, well-rounded bottom. An enigmatic gaze, a smile to lead a saint astray. A faithful replica of the real Marilyn whose triumph filled the world's cinema screens, whose every song was echoed by other singers and whose

famous walk was imitated by every aspiring film actress. The copy was more convincing than the real thing: the Marilyn without make-up, with pale lips, dark-circled eyes, silent and tense, who shrank back at the sight of her mirror image. I made my excuses to this glittering, counterfeit Marilyn and walked her back to her car before she had recognized the other, genuine one.

I still loved her. I never stopped loving her, both in her splendour and in her days of decline. Perhaps I should have been more possessive when she was mine or been able to win her back again once I had lost her? I shall never know the answer. I remember a long photo session – it must have been in the very early fifties – when she had realized her power over men. I was determined to keep my resolution, never again to be more than just a friend to her. She was posing on a bed, her hair in disorder, the sheets crumpled, just about to drink a glass of milk with a raw egg in it. The titillating contrast between the torrid moments evoked by the tumbled bedclothes and the wholesome purity of the milk and eggs had affected me. The heat of the spotlights, the fatigue induced by all those hours spent setting up the shots, the deliberately suggestive scene I had composed, created a disturbing intimacy between us. I tried to escape by fiddling around with my cameras, trying out new angles. But Marilyn seemed to want to play on this ambiguous atmosphere. She lay back indolently in the bed and closed her eyes, smiling as if at some memory, gave a soft sigh of luxurious languor, and of her own accord drew aside the sheet with deliberate provocation. Was it my pride which made me ignore her invitation? Or fear of spoiling that incomparable memory of our brief honeymoon in the snow for a passing moment's gratification?

I think I was right. It was the only way to keep my own special place in Marilyn's life, which no one suspected and no one could take away from me.

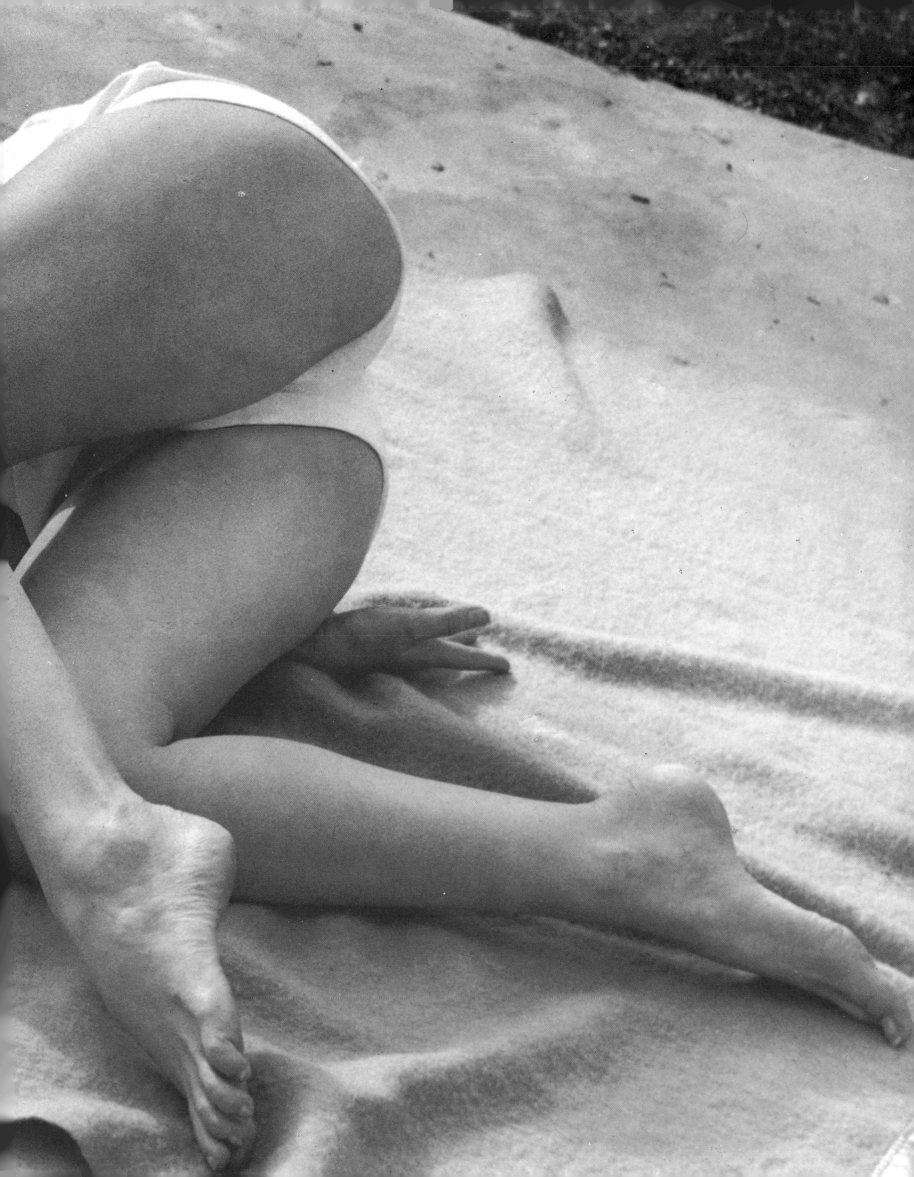

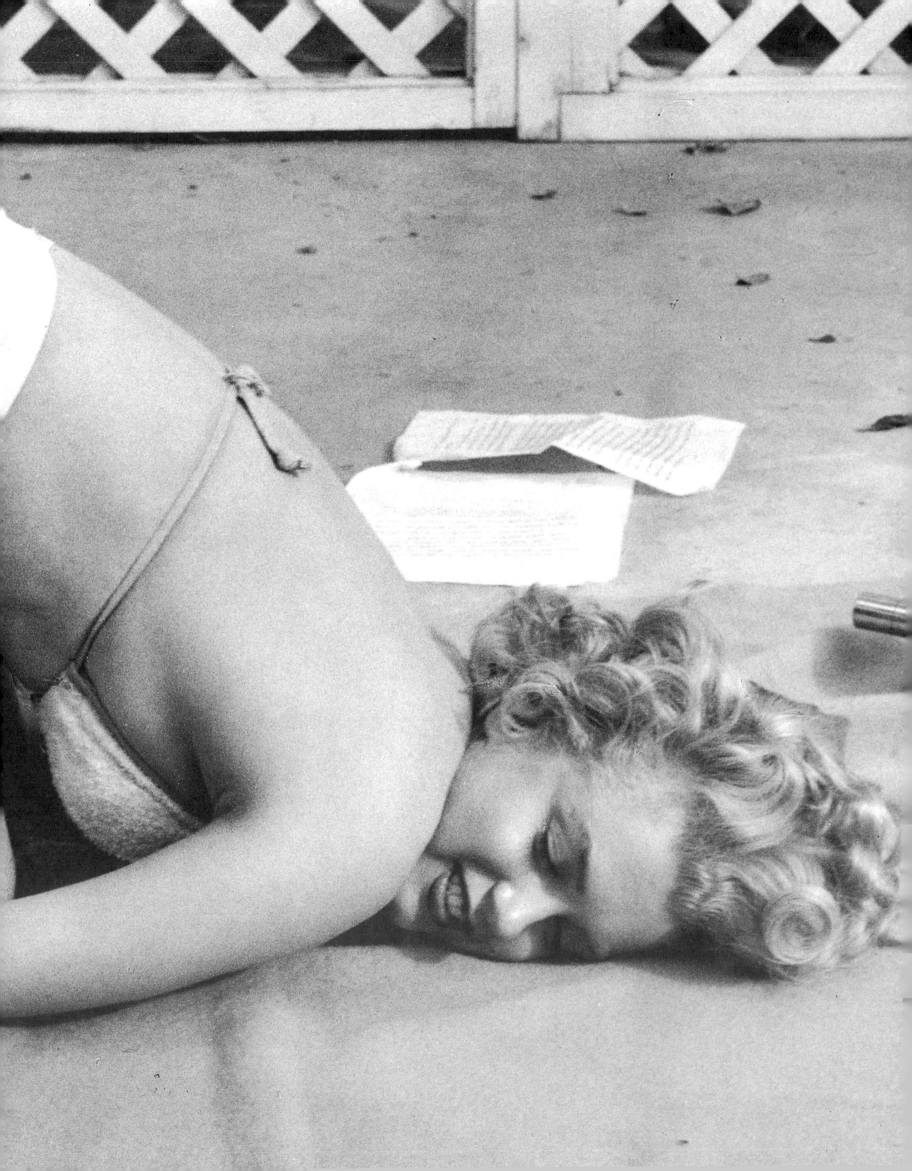

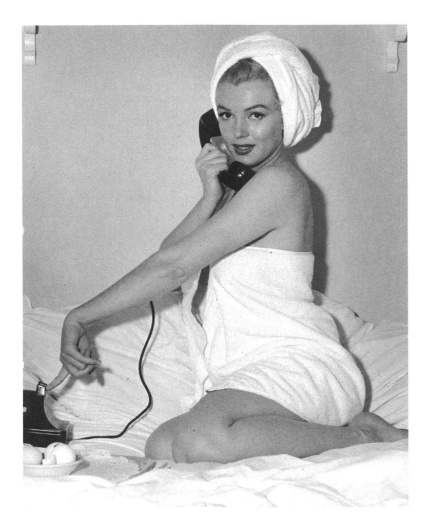 

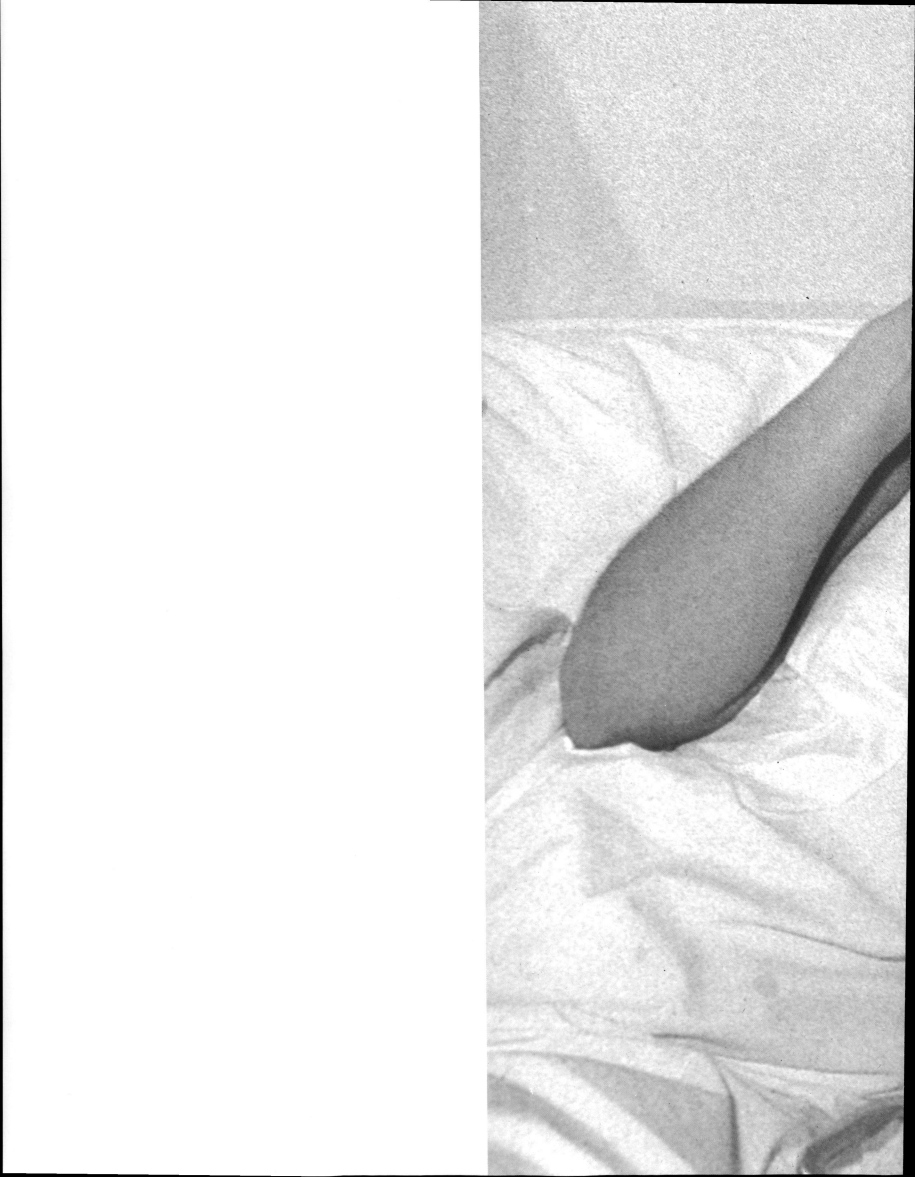

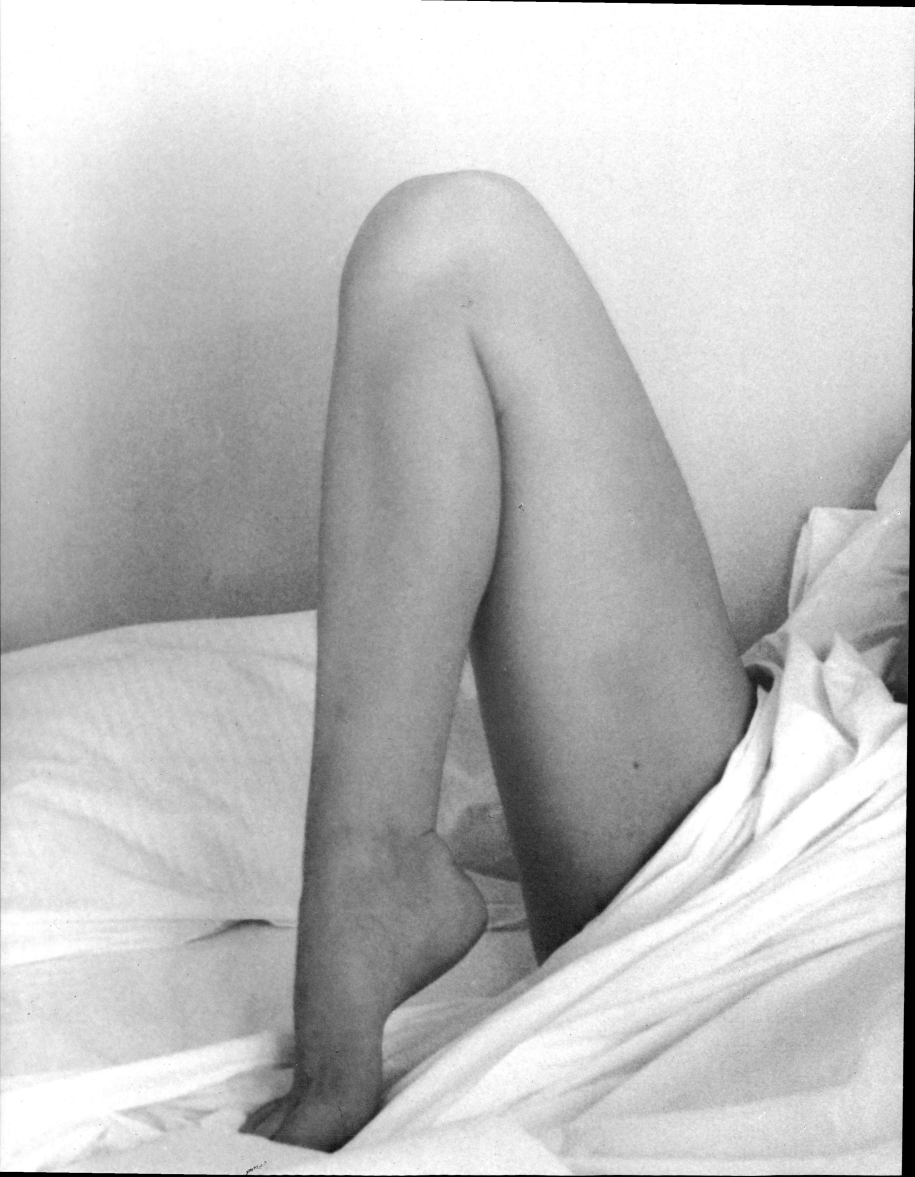

DANGER SIGNALS

Our next photo session was to prove even more disturbing for me. This time the cause was not the passing fancy of an over-indulged film star but the deep self-torment of a woman whom nothing could reassure, not even success. One night, shortly after the 'vamp' scene, Marilyn called me. It was two o'clock in the morning. She could not sleep. She was alone, unhappy, on the edge of despair. She wanted me to come and fetch her. She suggested we could take a series of photos with one of the darkened streets of Beverley Hills as a backdrop.

'Now?'

'Yes, right now.'

I would certainly have refused had I not caught a

A dark alley in Beverley Hills, 1953. André's last photos of Marilyn, taken by the light of his car headlights, seem to foreshadow her death nine years later

note of desperation in her voice which made my heart turn over. I got out of bed, grabbed my cameras and dashed off to join her.

She was not wearing any make-up. Her hair was dishevelled. She had dark-circled eyes. But if this was what she wanted . . . I tried to find the right lighting to soften her drawn features, to pick out some greenery to lessen the squalor of the dustbin-lined street where she had taken me. There was nothing. Was this sinister dead-end street how she saw her future? I dared not say anything. I wanted to give her a chance to express the anguish and despair which had overwhelmed her that night. Did she have a foreboding about some tragic event in her life? When we had finished she said to me in a barely audible voice: 'You usually write captions for your photos. You can put "The end of everything" underneath these.'

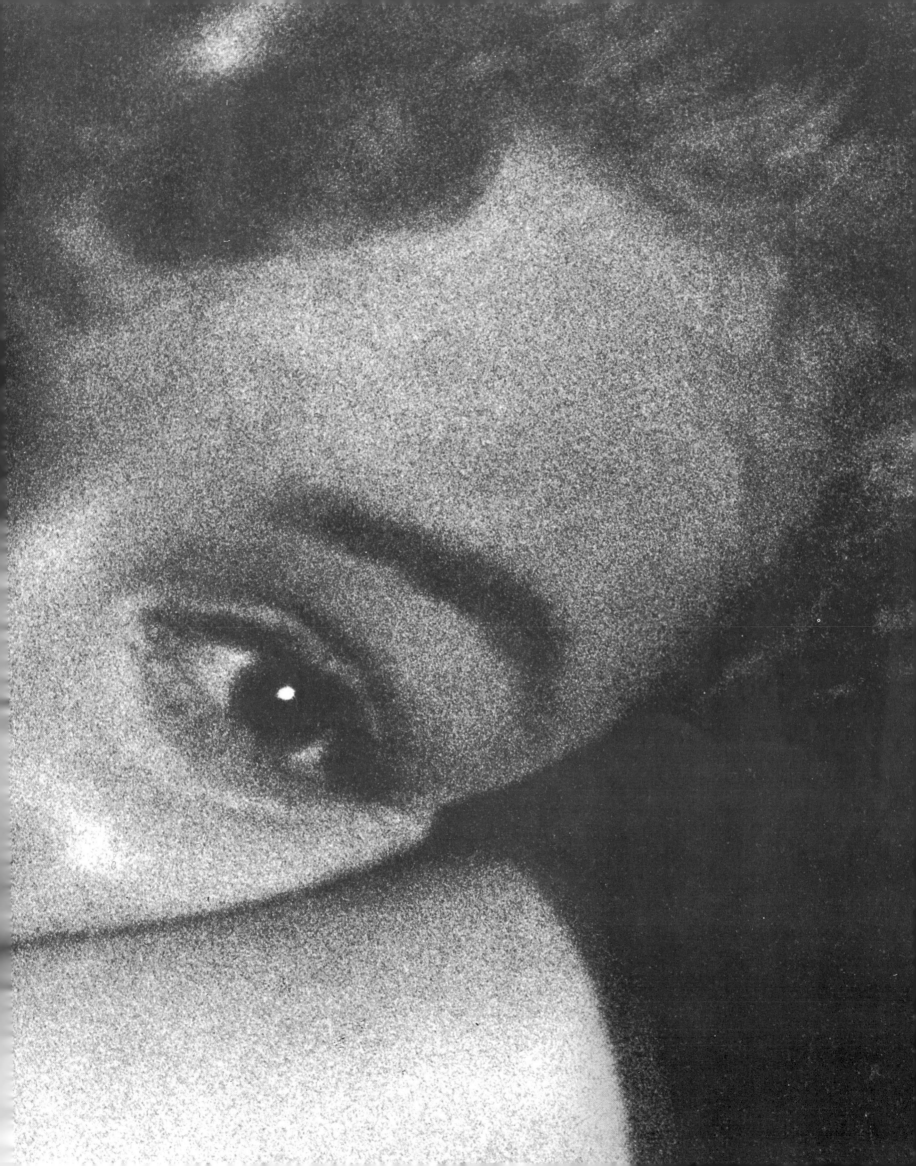

THE END OF EVERYTHING

her career had turned into an ordeal. The man who should have done his utmost to help, her husband Arthur Miller, had written a harrowing screenplay for her with a telling title: *The Misfits*. The atmosphere on location was fraught with tension. There was the heat and dust, and her co-stars were themselves contending with serious problems. Montgomery Clift could only just cope with life; Clark Gable felt threatened by illness, while his young wife was expecting a baby. Alone among the great Hollywood film directors, John Huston, ever watchful and perceptive of his cast's personalities, fortunately understood Marilyn's crippling insecurity. She was always late on set, and did not even show up at all some days; she forgot her lines. The entire cast, down to the smallest bit player, were exasperated by her. The film crew lost patience. The production team was horrified by the budget over-runs caused by the female star's instability. The press repeated the pitying or bitchy comments, expressing compassion for a sick, unbalanced Marilyn or criticizing her self-indulgent behaviour, unworthy of a professional.

I watched from afar as she slid into a private hell befogged by tranquillizers and a variety of sleeping pills. An idea had come to me for a 'Marilyn Album' of my close-ups, reflecting the often contradictory emotions which had moulded her features since she had first turned up on my doorstep in 1945. I planned to compose montages of her face against backgrounds of the desert, sea, mountains and forests to reflect each concept: hope, doubt, pain, death. Why had I got rid of so many boxes of negatives that day in a fit of depression, and buried them in a corner of my flooded garden? Without much hope I dug up the negatives I had so stupidly thrown away. Some were irretrievably damaged. Others could be salvaged. I wanted to compile a collection worthy of the woman who had been my muse. Some of these records of the past were particularly moving. Especially those where she was wearing no make-up, radiating enthusiastic joy like a little girl or, in stark contrast, possessed by a nameless foreboding.

One Friday in the fall of 1960, Marilyn turned up without warning. She was dressed in black and for the first time I noticed she no longer had that special glow of youth which only a short time before had made her so dazzling. She was well into her thirties. Insomnia, tension, the shock of Clark Gable's sudden death, her separation from Arthur Miller, had all left their mark. She was smiling, apparently calm, but I could tell she was on edge.

'If you're still so keen on taking photographs of me, go ahead. I'm free tomorrow, this evening, now this minute: suit yourself.'

Her tone was a bit curt and made me angry. I was looking forward to a well-earned weekend. I wanted to sleep, swim, have a good dinner in town, perhaps pick up a girl, anything but take photos.

I pointed to the papers piled high on my desk, the chairs, the bookshelves. There was work everywhere, even on the carpet. I was sick to death of it. She said she was sorry to have troubled me and left without even accepting a cup of tea.

I was ashamed of having been so boorish. I jumped into my car and headed for the Château Marmont where she was staying: an old-fashioned hotel, known for its restful atmosphere. Marilyn had a two-room suite there; there were trunks and cases everywhere. Had she just arrived or was she preparing to leave? I had been so off-hand that she had not had time to tell me. *The Misfits* was in the can; there was nothing else planned for her. She had decided to leave for New York without quite knowing why. Probably because she had no home of her own and made a habit of wandering from one hotel to another. Then she had decided against it – there was no point.

I realized she felt very alone, bereft; I was filled with anguish for her. To have striven so hard for all those years, only to end up with such emptiness! Had this loneliness driven her to come and see me on such a trivial pretext? She fetched a bottle of champagne from the refrigerator. And drank a glass of it in silence. For the first time we had nothing to say to each other. We were both of us worn out, ill at ease, lost for words. Had she come running to me, hoping I would take her in my arms? Why had I been unable to understand? I should have swept all those papers off my table, kindled a blazing fire, uncorked a bottle of good wine and proceeded to love her, just love her as if nothing else mattered and make her forget everything else.

Instead, I was in the impersonal surroundings of a luxury hotel, uneasy, not knowing what to do about this woman who haunted thousands of men's dreams, whom I had failed even to offer a shoulder to cry on. I remembered that during those far-off days together when she was tired after a long drive, or depressed by our distressing visit to her mother, I had made her laugh by telling her crazy stories. I felt I should return to my bad old ways.

When she had been hospitalized because of a nervous breakdown and was asked for the name of someone close to her to be informed in case of an emergency, she could think of no one. Not even me, I thought with a certain sadness. But this evening she had turned to me, I was the one to whom she was crying for help. So I hazarded the suggestion that we should go off together somewhere; how about my homeland, Transylvania? She listened to me as she had in the past. She smiled. That was already a modest victory. She was obviously exhausted. When I left her she seemed a little comforted – at least I thought so. When I telephoned her hotel the next morning, I was told she had just left to catch a flight to New York.

I last saw Marilyn alive on 1 June 1961. I was working outdoors when I suddenly remembered it was her birthday. I had read somewhere that she was at the Beverley Hills Hotel and, on the off chance, I dialled the number. They put me through to her room immediately. Without saying who it was, I started humming 'Happy Birthday . . . ' She interrupted me, sounding overjoyed.

'André, is that you? Come on over at once, let's celebrate!'

She was alone. On a little table beside some flowers she had placed a jar of caviar and two bottles of champagne. She seemed in very good form.

'What a relief,' she sighed. 'It's so good to have some peace and quiet.'

Fox had organized a cocktail party in her honour at the studios but she had only stayed a few minutes before pleading tiredness and leaving. No one had tried to stop her. They were used to her unpredictable behaviour.

'They're all against me. When I just can't take any more they think I'm being temperamental; they can't understand what it's like to be so tired that it's impossible to get out of bed in the morning.'

I knew only too well how badly she was sleeping, her whole nervous system was giving way. What really upset me about her wrecked life was her bitterness: her success was a sham, her hopes thwarted; she had been let down repeatedly, even by the men who had said they loved her. Her money had been squandered; fame had become a burden.

'They've all exploited me and now I've got nothing.'

But she was a star. People would help her go even further, attracted by her fame. Others would profit by her success. This is the way things are.

'For heaven's sake, Marilyn, it's not the end of the world.'

I said this in the same scolding yet cajoling manner she had once used to mollify me when I was complaining about having my camera and case stolen. What I was trying to do was convince her that she was still beautiful, more beautiful than anyone else as far as most men were concerned, and certainly for me.

I could see that the cover had been thrown back from the bed in the next room; I took her in my arms, searching for her lips. I lost my head. She cried out, protesting:

'Oh please, don't! I'm so tired of all that . . . Don't ask anything of me, you of all people.'

Her eyes were full of tears. I felt I had been a brute. I knew she had only just left hospital after a major operation. I was ashamed of myself. I said goodbye and left her in peace. Outside the night air smelled good. A doubt assailed me. Was she making a fool of me? There had been so much talk. Perhaps she had got rid of me because she was expecting someone else? I retraced my steps. Her bedroom light went out almost immediately. I stood watching the white curtains of her window, overcome with remorse at my suspicions.

The next day I sent her a basket of her favourite fruit and before she left for Hollywood she left a bouquet outside my door: a selection of her latest photos. Smiling, radiant – utterly misleading. I little guessed that this was our last goodbye.

André de Dienes

Hollywood, October 1984

We would like to thank the following for their help:

Michel Assouline
Prosper Assouline
Suzanne Chantal
Jean-François Cholet
Eric Colmet Daage
Anne Davis
Kalman de Dienes
Nicolas Hugnet
Brigitte Logeart
Jean-Jacques Naudet
and Gary Newman